THE ART OF SELFLESS SERVICE

A Biographical Account of the Public Service Career of
Mr. Akinwunmi D. Ambode

Safari Books Ltd
Ibadan

Mr. Akin Ambode

Akin Ambode is a Public Finance Management Expert and the Chief Executive Officer of Brandsmiths Consulting Limited – a public finance and management-consulting firm with deep knowledge of the Nigerian public sector. He is a former Accountant General of Lagos State serving in that capacity between 2006 and 2012, he served in several other capacities including Permanent Secretary Ministry of Finance, Auditor General for Local Government and across all cadres of Lagos state's civil service for a total of 27 years before his voluntary retirement in 2012.

He gained recognition for outstanding excellence by the Joint Tax Board (JTB)/FIRS on the successful organization of the 1st National Tax Retreat in Nigeria in 2005.

Akin is an alumnus of Wharton Business School Advance Management Programme. He has attended courses at several renowned institutions including Cranfield School of Management, Cranfield, England, the Institute of Management Development Lausanne, Switzerland, INSEAD Singapore and the Harvard Kennedy School of Government, Boston, USA. He holds a Masters degree in Accounting (Financial Management) and a B.Sc. degree in Accounting from the University of Lagos, he is a Hubert Humphrey Fellow in Accounting and Finance from Boston University, Boston Massachusetts, United States. He is also a Fellow of the Institute of Chartered Accountants of Nigeria (ICAN).

Akin believes in mentoring and sees it as an effective way of helping people to develop and progress in their chosen careers and making sure they maximize their potentials.

He is the founder of the La Roche Leadership Foundation, a foundation that he founded in 2012 to attend to the well being and prosperity of Nigerian students in all facets of their educational endeavours, be it technical, formal, social or vocational and to create and sustain a positive, enabling and empowering educational environment for children and young people. Akin, himself having been a beneficiary of two prestigious scholarships, the Federal Government Scholarship award for postgraduate studies in 1987 and the Fulbright scholarship in 1998.

He is the current National President of the Federal Government College Warri Old Students Association (FEGOCOWOSA).

Another passion Akin has is his love for entertainment and the Nigerian entertainment industry. He believes that the entertainment industry can be a powerful voice to drive positive change in the society and economy. He has established long-standing relationships with a number of artists and supported them in various ways to inspire and stimulate innovation in the local and international entertainment space.

Published by
Safari Books Ltd
Ile Ori Detu
1, Shell Close
Onireke, Ibadan.
Email: safarinigeria@gmail.com

© Marina Osoba

Publisher: Chief Joop Berkhout, *OON*
Deputy Publisher: George Berkhout
Editor: Odetola Olalekan

Cover Design: *www.printassure.com*
Photography: Hantara Pictures

First published 2014

All rights reserved. This book is copyright and so no part of it may be reproduced, stored in a retrieval system, or transmitted, in any form or by any means, electronic, mechanical, electrostatic, magnetic tape, photocopying, recording or otherwise, without the prior written permission of the author.

ISBN: 978-978-8431-42-8

Dedication

To all public servants who have continually served selflessly, but never had a voice.

In loving memory of
Nelson Rolihlahla Mandela;
an embodiment of selfless service.

Contents

Dedication   v
Foreword   ix
Prologue   xiii

Chapter One
Born to Serve, Learning Early to Run   1

Chapter Two
The Federal Government College, Warri Years   5

Chapter Three
Journey to Manhood   15

Chapter Four
Start of A Career   21

Chapter Five
Multi-Tasking Thrives!   29

Chapter Six
The Local Government Years; Grassroots and Loving It   35

Chapter Seven
The Hubert Humphrey Scholar Awakens   41

Chapter Eight

Resolving to Innovate, Ready to Serve … 49

Chapter Nine

The State Service … 53

Chapter Ten

Making a Difference; the Reluctant Role Model … 61

Chapter Eleven

A Man of Numbers … 75

Chapter Twelve

Still the Same Person … 81

Chapter Thirteen

The Renaissance Man … 87

Chapter Fourteen

Exceptional Extracurricular Expeditions … 93

Chapter Fifteen

The Bare Essentials … 103

Epilogue … 113

Index of Quotations … 117

Acknowledgements … 119

Foreword

The key reason that I feel qualified to write this foreword is my fairly close interaction with the subject of this book. Akinwunmi Ambode is definitely a beacon of service and is therefore fully qualified to give us an insight on how to provide selfless service.

This is a book about a journey from childhood to manhood and how experiences in life have defined and refined the concept of serving others. All the chapters of the book are peppered with quotes from statesmen and notable writers and this sets the stage for a very interesting chronology of remarkable events in this outstanding Nigerian's life.

The early chapters trace Akinwunmi Ambode's birth into a strong Christian family and his dogged determination to succeed, culminating in excellent results in his common entrance exams.

His experience at Federal Government College Warri was clearly a defining period for him and it largely moulded him into the person he is today. Akinwunmi says Warri taught him the importance of integrity, imbibing the wholeness of honesty, dignity, discipline, diligence and selfless service. It is instructive that this Federal Unity School played such a decisive role in the life of Akinwunmi Ambode, yet it is the same Unity Schools that are now a shadow of themselves. They no longer command the reverence that comforted Akinwunmi's father to telegraph his son all the way from Lagos to Warri to get a first class education.

Again, the value of a well-grounded foundation began to shine through in Akinwunmi's higher education in the University of Lagos and the start of his career in the Lagos State Public Service. Yes, the infrastructure of F.G.C Warri and University of Lagos were adjudged first class, but it is clear from his various experiences that Akinwunmi was also destined to succeed through sheer doggedness and a sense of purpose. Hear him in chapter four when he said "the time had come for him to move forward with his academic plan. One year after he started as an Accountant Grade 2 in the Lagos State Waste Disposal Board, Akin went ahead and registered for both his ICAN Certification and his Masters Degree programme at the University of Lagos."

An important lesson that we can also all learn from this book is the Author's emphasis on his ability to multi-task so early in his career. This is a skill that is so lacking in many of us today as we can only efficiently do one thing at a time. This multi-tasking skill probably accounts for his fast track rise in the public service to Accountant-General that is clearly depicted in chapter six of the book.

There is a huge devotion in chapter seven and eight to Akinwunmi's experience as a Hubert Humphrey School and its impact on his outlook to the public service. Perhaps the best chapters for me are nine and ten which describe his switch from the Local Government Service to the State and the testimonies of some of the staff whose lives he had touched. It is often said that the best gift you can give to another person is your ability to positively touch that person's life. This is clearly demonstrated in the vivid testimonies given by those who worked with him. Akinwunmi's towering influence in his various old students Association's also clearly demonstrates his unique ability to touch other people's lives.

Akinwunmi was very correct, when he had this to say in his opening chapter:

> "In other words, we must measure our worth by the amount of service, selfless service we put into our families, our work place and colleagues therein, our society, our country, our world. This is our true worth, serving selflessly everyday for the good of all men, whether we get remembered or not."

This is a quintessential book about a first class Nigerian who has dedicated a large part of his life to serving others selflessly and with humility. It is a book that should not be ignored.

Adeniji Kazeem esq.
December 2013.

Prologue

"As to the kindness you mention, I wish I could have been of more service to you than I have been, but if I had, the only thanks that I should desire are that you would always be ready to serve any other person that may need your assistance, and so let good offices go around, for mankind are all of a family. As for my own part, when I am employed in serving others, I do not look upon myself as conferring favours, but paying debts."

– Benjamin Franklin.

What is service? So many definitions come to mind, but simply put, service is being a servant, working in employment for the good of another. Selfless service can be defined therefore as performing service for the good of others, not seeking or expecting benefit for oneself, but acknowledgement of the Creator's free gift of talent and opportunities.

To be selfless in service takes a lot, it takes courage; because most times, the magnitude of what needs to be done can be daunting, it takes time; things once started must be seen through to a conclusive end no matter how long that takes. It takes effort; the easy way out always leads to mediocrity and mediocrity never suffices, it takes persistence; because life has a way of throwing up road blocks in the most unexpected ways. It takes patience and focus; because things never go the way we plan them; life throws us curve balls and we need to roll with the punches. It takes love and charity; no one can serve without loving the people that you serve even when they are unlovable and cruelly criticize everything, without looking at the merits of one's vision. Moreover it takes vision; because one must see the end from the beginning, so to speak. In other words, selfless service is indeed an art; it takes a unique marriage of the head, heart and hands to pull it off successfully.

The art of selfless service is what everyone who truly wants to serve must master and practice. In the world today, selfless service is fast becoming a lost art. The pressure of living in today's world is such that the self is the centre of all accomplishments and must get all the accolades. Today's self is covetous, selfish, petulant, self seeking, adores grandstanding, is unnecessarily sensitive, easily offended, always dissatisfied, is unsympathetic, unhappy, ungrateful and is always in competition with everyone. The attention seeking self hates to share the spotlight with anyone; it abhors the acknowledgement of anyone else but the all important self. Yet if we consider the antecedence of self, we discover that it was someone else's selfless service that created the conditions necessary for others who came later to survive and thrive.

This means that if there is to be continuity, progress and growth, selfless service is not negotiable, it must come naturally, it must be sustained, it must be intensified and it must be the hallmark of what we do and who we are. For our worth cannot be measured by what material things we own, but by the work we do and how we do it. In other words, we must measure our worth by the amount of service, selfless service we put into our families, our work place and colleagues therein, our society, our country, our world. This is our true worth, serving selflessly everyday for the good of all men, whether we get remuneration or not.

This book aims to show how to accomplish the art of selfless service, by examining and following the footsteps of a man who made a pact with his Creator to serve selflessly, giving of himself and asking that everyone return the favour by serving yet another. Akinwunmi Ambode does not seek for sainthood, titles, thanks or any recognition, he is motivated to allow his story to be told simply to show that it can be done, one person, anybody can make a difference, have an impact, touch humanity and change society. For as he says:

> *"...If we seek recompense for everything we do for others, imagine what we owe those who have done so much for us? Who can repay our God for His manifold mercies that we enjoy everyday; the air we breathe, the clean water we drink, the cool breezes that blow, the sky above, the earth below? Who can repay one's*

parents for coming into this world? Who can repay those who have fought for the freedoms we enjoy?"

A thought worth pondering.
So, in the words of Henry Drummond,

"...you will find as you look back upon your life, that the moments that stand out are the moments when you have done things for others..."

CHAPTER ONE

Born to Serve and Learning Early to Run

"Between the innocence of babyhood and the dignity of manhood we find a delightful creature called a boy. Boys come in assorted sizes, weights and colours, but all boys have the same creed: to enjoy every second of every minute of every hour of everyday and to protest with noise (their only weapon)..."
— *Alan Beck.*

Akinwunmi Ambode came into this world at Epe General Hospital, Epe in Lagos State on the 14th of June, 1963, the sixth child in a family of ten children. As his parents welcomed the newest member of their family into the world, little did they know that baby Akin would, as some children do, bring his special brand of service to the family. The Ambode family being Christian, Yoruba and having a unique blend of traditional and contemporary views, always taught that age and status in the family must be respected. Akin's upbringing therefore did not differ in this respect and from an early age he was taught the importance of family values, service and humility being very important.

Shortly thereafter, the family moved from the serene and peaceful Epe to the hustle and bustle of Lagos Mainland. The vibrancy of his new home and surroundings meant that he needed protection at such an early age. His older siblings readily took him under their wings, as the situation demanded. The Ambode family soon settled into their routine in their new home and baby Akin grew into his place in the family, learning family values, Yoruba traditions and Christian precepts as did the other children.

As the sixth child in a family with many boys, he learnt at an early age the value of bonding and team work. His family unit was close and loving, each person looking out for the other. Family life was fun, warm, nurturing and protective; a hard-working father who doted on his children, but didn't spoil them, a loving and caring mother who saw that needs were met in that nurturing motherly way and in this environment, he blossomed. There was plenty of play but having older siblings really jump started his learning experience, as interaction with his family opened up the world of books, reading, learning and exploration.

He started school life at St. Jude's Primary School, Ebute Metta, in January 1969. Being of small stature and very young, even then, he knew that he was growing up in a family where education is valued as a priority, so he was a serious student from the beginning. Going to St. Jude's was like embarking on a voyage of discovery; from getting dressed in the mornings in his school uniform, taking the trip to school, meeting up with classmates and teachers and entering the world of learning, school was always an interesting part of Akin's life in Ebute Metta. His fondness for school was matched by impressive results and a dedication to school work that seemed ahead of young Akin's abilities for his age, but he took it all in his stride; his older siblings helping to get him to push his boundaries.

As months and years passed by, the little boy who started out eagerly and enthusiastically got to primary five, doing so well that his parents decided to allow him sit the Common Entrance examination in that class. Perhaps they thought the experience would serve him well when he got to class six and never thought that he would actually make the cut, but when the results came out he surprised everyone. A gifted and intelligent student, he passed his Common Entrance with flying colours. Having done so well, his parents were reluctant to let him go, but had no choice than to encourage him to take the next step and thus open a new chapter in his life.

A few years before, the government's new educational policy, the Unity School programme that brought children from the different parts of Nigeria to one of three locations: Sokoto in the North, Okposi in the East (later moved to Enugu as a result of the Civil War from 1967-1970) and Warri in the then Mid-West, was conceptualized and became a reality. These schools took only the very best students from around the country and Akin received his letter, inviting him to attend secondary school at Federal Government College, Warri.

Initially, the very thought that their young son would leave the home and his state and head for a far and unknown place disconcerted the household. There were no family members living in Warri who would act as guardians for the young boy; he would be the first child in the family to leave the security and protection of home to go so far away to school; it would be the first time he was away from home.

The decision was a hard one to make, but the die was cast, Akin was going to Warri. His father would have preferred a school nearer home, and no doubt his mother must have thought along the lines of Angelo Patri:

> *"...I have a boy to bring up. Help me send him into the world with a mission of service. Strengthen my mind and heart that I may teach him that he is his brother's keeper. Grant that he may serve those who know not the need of service, and not knowing, need it the most. I have a boy to bring up. So guide and direct me that I may do this service to the glory of God, the service of my country, and to my son's happiness."*

CHAPTER TWO

The Federal Government College, Warri Years

"...the entire object of true education is to make people not merely to do the right things, but enjoy them; not merely industrious, but to love industry; not merely learned, but to love knowledge; not merely pure, but to love purity; not merely just, but to hunger and thirst after justice..."
— John Ruskin.

There were few things in life scarier than travelling to Warri in the 1970's especially if you were just eleven years old and had lived all your life in Lagos. Nothing could have prepared Akin for the dense forests, the long tiring road trip and the anxiety of knowing that he was going to be separated from his family for months on end in a strange and new environment and without a familiar face. Nevertheless, he was more excited than afraid; new friends were waiting to be made, a new school waiting to be conquered, new teachers to learn from, a new town to be explored; Warri was going to be fun, whether he liked it or not.

Right from the first day, Akin made up his mind that his experience at Warri had to count, and count it did. The man, who would make his years at Warri the best in his life thus far, was a retired British Major who had worked in Education in the Colonial Administration at King's College, Lagos and in post Independence Nigeria at Federal Government Colleges in Sokoto and Warri. Mr. Philip Howard Davis (Papa as he was called by all the students) was in a class of his own. A brilliant, passionate disciplinarian, he single-handedly inspired generations of students who passed through his hands at all the schools he administered. Akin was about to meet and be touched by Papa.

The school year in 1974 had just been changed from running from January to December to the internationally recognized September to June, so in September of 1974, Akin left for Warri to start the next chapter of his life as a student of Federal Government College, Warri in the then Mid-Western State of Nigeria.

As expected, he made lots of new friends from all over Nigeria at Warri, all of who have remained close friends to date. Warri was a great melting pot; all tribes, religions, social groups, cultures and traditions, all in the sanctity of the hallowed walls of Federal Government College Warri under the tutelage of some of the best teachers in the country and most of all, under the able administration of Philip Howard Davis. This was a match made in heaven. To understand the metamorphosis of Akin in this unique environment, a little background about this school has to be given.

Education at Federal Government College, Warri was not just academic, P. H. Davis believed in a holistic approach which would imbue the child in every facet of learning. He was probably ahead of his peers in Nigeria and most of the world in this regard. He believed in producing the 'total child'; a child that is academically, emotionally, socially, culturally and spiritually sound. He also realized that it was important that the Sciences were given extra resources because as a developing country, Nigeria badly needed future giants in Science. To that end, an annual Science Fair was held at which each year of study was encouraged to produce a scientific project to present during the fair. In 1978, Form 2 students produced a solar powered water heater which supplied hot water to the Biology and Chemistry Labs for well over eight years. This environment created the 'Can do' attitude that Akin is well known for, he innovates and adapts to whatever environment he finds himself in.

The school had four houses, first known by letters of the alphabet and later by the names: Unity, Independence, School and National houses. The infrastructure of the school was excellent, facilities well maintained and regularly upgraded. There were a plethora of foreign teachers under P. H. Davis then, who with their equally excellent Nigerian colleagues, made the school the giant it then was in academics.

Being a retired military man who had served under the systems created by Lord Lugard, P. H. Davis was a great believer in the place of sports in the development of the total child. As such, sports were a big part of life at the College. Endurance treks, track and field, volleyball, basketball, lawn tennis, badminton, football, hockey, cricket and the little known tennicourt were taught and played with so much enthusiasm that the school was regularly visited by Sports officials from the then Bendel State Sports Council to scout for talents. The College was also the place that University of Benin came to look for gifted sports students in their final year of study, who would be given priority when it came to university placement.

Akin loved sports; he played what was lovingly referred to as 'local Wembley', that is, informal 'five a-side' football matches between the different houses, he was on the school's hockey team and cricket teams and played as a member of these school teams around the country, and has the distinction of playing cricket for the then Bendel State as a member of the Bendel State Cricket team while he was a student at the College.

The 'total child' concept was carried further by Davis into the social life of the school with the creation of clubs and societies that students had to be a part of. The uniformed clubs were the Boy Scouts, Girl Guides, Red Cross and Man-O-War. Others were the Literary & Debating Society, Drama club, Press club, Young Scientists' club, Jet club, Chess club, U.N.E.S.C.O club amongst others. There was entertainment every Saturday, ranging from film shows, dances, quiz nights, Girls' night, Form Four night, Lower Six night, etc. Akin was a member of several societies particularly the Literary and Debating Society.

The spiritual life of the students was not left out. There were Anglican and Catholic services on Sunday mornings and on Fridays Muslim students were taken to the Mosque in Warri Township. Also, there were prayer meetings during the week and a strong presence of the Scripture Union. Prayer was a big part of the life of the school. Before and after meals and after assembly the school was led in prayer by the prefects on duty. This instilled in Akin a strong sense of spirituality, integrity and morality as a member of the Anglican Communion of the school.

To introduce students to the concept of Democracy and Leadership and serve as a mouth piece for students, the School Authorities introduced the Students' Representative Council (SRC), a body made up of elected students who represented the students' voices at School Administration Meetings. They were grouped into Committees such as the Entertainment Committee (of which Akin served the school during his A' Levels as the Entertainment Committee Chairman in charge of the entertainment, every weekend and public holidays, of a school population of nearly one thousand students), Health Committee, Publicity Committee and others and were responsible for the work their committees did. P. H. Davis was preparing the students for the coming democracy which then was just a pipe dream, given the entrenchment of the military in the governance of the country.

As regards discipline and leadership, P. H. Davis, a retired Major of the British Army, was not one to condone any form of indiscipline. He was something of a benevolent father with those who were meek and obedient, but with the stubborn and naughty, he brought the full weight of his military training to bear. There was a popular maxim at Warri; *'Obey before you complain'* and this was followed to the letter. Thus the school had a chain of command which was strictly observed, Akin found the discipline instilled at home and at the College made him grow and mature and serve well. In his later years, he served as a School Prefect and part of that chain of command; he was much like P. H. Davis, well loved by junior students, appreciated by fellow Prefects, Teachers and Housemasters, feared by the bullies, the disobedient and the rule breakers.

The cultural life of the students was not ignored either. Every year, a festival of Arts and Culture was held in the school with the students competing for their respective houses, to celebrate their African Heritage. Plays were acted, poetry recited; traditional songs and dances with a full accompaniment of traditional musical instruments displayed and all these were assessed by a panel of judges that earned the winning house a trophy. For a colonial officer who had seen the greatness of the British Empire dismantling in the newly liberated former colony, P. H. Davis knew that Nigerian children had to be proud of their heritage to be authentic. Again, as expected of every student, Akin fully participated for his house in all these activities, enjoying the experience of all the many cultures and traditions that Warri had to offer, not just limited to the three major tribes, but also embracing the culture and traditions of the various minorities that made up the very diverse student body.

The spirit of brotherhood went beyond just the walls of the school itself. The roots of the present Unity Schools Old Students Association (USOSA) were sown decades ago when students of different Unity Schools visited each other regularly for sports competitions, quizzes, debates and so on. Akin went for many of such excursions for sports competitions, Literary and Debating Society excursions and so on.

It was P. H. Davis, the ubiquitous and legendary 'Papa', who has the singular honour and distinction of being the longest serving, (15 years at Warri alone) most beloved and best Principal of the school to date, who put the school on the world map. It was under his administration that F.G.C. Warri became the best secondary institution in West Africa and ninth best in the world as judged then by U.N.E.S.C.O in a report on the state of education worldwide and based on W.A.E.C. O'Level and A' Level results of the 70's.

In 1981, after spending seven years in Warri completing his O'Levels and A' Levels, Akin had the distinction of achieving the second best result in West Africa in the Social Sciences, a great feat by any standards. He offered three subjects at A' Levels, getting an 'A' in Geography, a 'B' in Economics and a B in History and had the second best result in Nigeria, following after Prof. Fidelis Oditah (QC, SAN) also an old student of Warri.

Warri taught him the importance of integrity; imbibing the wholeness of honesty, dignity, discipline, diligence and selfless service. He learnt that the foundation his family had given him of bonding with like minds and working as a team player was invaluable to him during his Warri experience and he further built on that foundation. Akin also learnt in Warri that tribe is just a word; it does not define anyone and the negative stereotyping which was common place was bigotry at best. He had lived in close quarters with Nigerians of every tribe, shade and creed and found that the brotherhood at Warri broke down all barriers. He also learnt that his female classmates worked just as hard as his male classmates and were capable of doing just as well; this made him realize that women can be just as good as men and gave him a healthy respect for their abilities. Above all, his years at Warri gave him a most precious gift; the gift of brotherhood; of strong friendships that have endured to this day. It was these friendships that were soon to be tested.

Unfortunately and without warning, he lost his beloved father just two weeks after his eighteenth birthday and three weeks before his amazing result was released. The blow of losing his father at this stage in his life had a huge impact on him. Losing any parent is a disastrous event especially as a youth; the experience always touches the rest of one's life. It was a great loss in more ways than one; and one that would put all plans in jeopardy. (May his gentle soul rest in peace by His grace.)

For any young man, losing a father robs him of the first mentor of his life in so many ways. This loss would have far reaching consequences and create a new set of challenges. This loss however taught him a great lesson; that he would never be alone in good times, but he had loyal 'brothers' especially in bad times. The friends he made at Warri were to rally around him at this most painful time and help him get through the untimely loss of his father. Being an introvert, the quality of Akin's friends more than made up for their quantity and their loyalty and caring persuaded him in the belief of the need to nurture social capital. This early investment in social capital was to yield good dividends as it has become one of the hallmarks of Akin's life and remains one of the concepts that he believes in; that good, trusted and loyal friends are necessary in one's life. Akin found out the true value of friendship as aptly put by Frank Dempster Sherman in his poem titled 'A Prayer':

*"It is my joy in life to find,
In every turning of the road,
The strong arm of a comrade kind
To help me onward with my load.*

*And since I have no gold to give,
And love alone must make amends,
My only prayer is while I live,
God make me worthy of my friends."*

CHAPTER THREE

The Journey to Manhood

"We are put here to grow, and we ought to grow, and to use all the means of growth according to the laws of our being. The only real satisfaction there is, is to be growing up inwardly all the time, becoming just, true, generous, simple, manly, womanly, kind, active. And this can we all do, by doing each day the day's work as well as we can…"
— *James Freeman Clarke.*

In 1981, just months after the loss of his father, Akin found himself facing the unfolding of another chapter of his life. Not knowing what would happen as regards his education, the family having lost their sole breadwinner, Akin was at a crossroads; he had the opportunity to study a great many courses either in the

Arts or Social Sciences and had applied for Accountancy (first choice) and Law (second choice) to the University of Lagos at Akoka in Yaba, Lagos. The choice of the University of Lagos was not a coincidence; having spent seven years at Warri and losing his father so unexpectedly, Akin opted to be close to family and home.

Unilag, (as it is colloquially known) is another prestigious institution and although not the oldest tertiary institution in Nigeria, has carved an enviable niche for itself. Situated in the commercial powerhouse and what was then the country's administrative capital, Unilag would prove to be a tough challenge. Of the thousands that apply every year, only the very best got entry and were able to graduate from its Faculty of Business Administration and Akin knew that gaining entry to study Accountancy was not going to be a free pass to graduate three years later. It was definitely going to take more than just a great A' Level result to be able to wear an academic gown and hold a degree three years later, but fortunately for him, his Warri experience had prepared him for just such a challenge.

The University of Lagos was similar to Federal Government College, Warri in the sense that it is an institution that has good infrastructure, great Lecturers and a good atmosphere for learning in spite of the fact that its situation might cause many to think that the distractions of the city of Lagos would impede scholarship. However, in spite of the assumed notoriety of the city and without his father's love, guidance and finance, Akin buckled down and supported by a strong family bond, he found out that intelligence alone was not going to get him through. It was Unilag that taught him that hardwork entailed hours and hours of dedicated study, serious research and total dedication to his chosen course, not to mention that if one wanted to graduate with a good result, it would mean sacrificing the immediate gratification of partying and socializing.

1981 to 1984 were years of silent, yet steady growth and Akin threw himself into them, making sure that they counted for something. The teenager quietly became a man and then a university graduate, leaving the University with an impressive honours degree in Accountancy at the young age of 21.

As with all Nigerian graduates, Akin went home to await his call up to National Service in 1984. When his posting came, it could not have been more exciting, Akin had been posted to Sokoto in Sokoto State for his National Youth Service Corp year, in the extreme North West of the country. Once again, he would leave family and home and head to the unknown. The difference this time was that his years at Warri had prepared him for this kind of situation. He packed up and left for this new challenge.

Sokoto was a blessing in disguise; it afforded Akin the opportunity to reconnect with former students of his Warri days which made the whole experience invaluable. When orientation camp was over, he found himself posted to serve at the State branch of the Central Bank of Nigeria. This opened up a whole new horizon as he not only learnt more about Accountancy, but also discovered the intricacies of working in the Public Service.

Even as a Youth Corper, working in the Sokoto State branch of the Central Bank of Nigeria presented its own set of challenges. It was not one of those postings where one can hope to be ignored while the regular staff goes about doing the hardwork. He soon realized that his Corp year was not going to be an extended holiday. Right from the first day, Akin was thrown in at the deep end, but he was prepared for the challenge because of all the grooming that he had been through. Added to this was that on arrival, he met up with another former student of Warri, resident at the time in Sokoto, who offered him room and board for his entire service year. This meant that he could focus on learning more about working in the Public Service and he could put all the theory of his Accountancy course work at Unilag into practise. Not to mention that his living conditions were top notch, living way above what the usual Corper would experience.

The year in Sokoto offered several lessons; firstly, that social capital was still worth investing in; good friends are precious and should be treasured, secondly, that Accountancy was not only the right career choice for him, but had the potential to take him places and thirdly, that developing a diligent work ethic early in life makes any challenge surmountable. A man had come into his manhood and was ready to take on the world.

"Life is neither a banquet nor a dreary pilgrimage; it is neither a trading concern where all dividends that are fairly earned are punctually paid, nor a lotus-eater's paradise; it is a school of manhood."

– Burnett .H. Streeter.

CHAPTER FOUR

Start of a Career

"One thing I am resolved upon: I will not be a sponge or a parasite. I will give an honest equivalent for what I get. I want no man's money for which I have not rendered a full return. I want no wages that I have not earned. If I work for any man, or any company or any institution, I will render a full, ample, generous service. If I work for the city, state or the nation, I will give my best thought, my best effort, my most conscientious and efficient endeavor. No man, no body of men shall ever be made poor by their dealings with me. If I can give a little more than I can get everytime, in that shall be my happiness. The great commonwealth of human society shall not be the loser through me. I will take good care to put into the common fund more than I take out."

– Washington Gladden.

The National Youth Service Corp year inevitably came to an end and on passing out in June 1985, Akin found himself armed with all the necessary documentation and an immense hunger to take the next step; starting his career in Accountancy. Back to Lagos in July 1985, the usual rituals of the newly released Corpers took place; newspapers were scoured for vacancies, applications were written, interviews were attended and favours were called in. Yet for all the impressive results and beautifully written recommendations, nothing was forthcoming on the job front. Akin found himself in a quandary with nothing to do. For someone who thrives on structure, routine and the love of being productive, this state of joblessness was totally unacceptable. After pounding the pavement relentlessly job hunting and finding nothing, he was perplexed. Inactivity was taking its toll and surely enough, Akin found he was slipping into frustration.

It was at this point that he had an epiphany of sorts; Akin left the job hunting aside and started his search for meaning in his life. This brought him to a deep spiritual place where he rededicated himself to God. He cut out several habits and became serious with his Christian walk. He became a changed person. This experience helped him to prioritize and his purpose crystallized into a clear vision for his life.

He reconnected with family; this had always been the bedrock of his upbringing, but the separations from home and family caused breaches which always had to be bridged, and the family always provided a safe haven when he returned to them. He found out that one always needs people, especially those at the very heart of one's existence.

He also rediscovered the art of selflessly serving others, not seeking anything in return. It was a major turning point in his personal life and set him on a path of wanting to serve in any way he could be of assistance. There was a new purpose for his life and it was not the pursuit of accolades, material wealth and creature comforts; taking the focus off his wants had allowed him to realistically evaluate himself and make adjustments. This was the beginning of his habit of regular introspection; even till now, from time to time, he takes time off and examines his successes and failures. This helps him to ensure that he remains true to what his ideals, principles and conscience dictate. It was a good starting point to build a career on.

It was a family member who incidentally put Akin on the path to Public Service. There were several vacancies for newly graduated Accountants that had recently appeared in one of the dailies and he was advised to apply. Although Akin had hoped for a job to come through in the private sector, perhaps something in an Accounting firm or a financial institution, especially as all his friends who had studied Accountancy like he did, were now working for banks, insurance houses and other financial institutions, he found that those doors were not opening for him. At this time, most young people did not want to work in the public service, the pay was abysmally poor, the conditions of work were outdated, the bureaucracy stifling, the future was not attractive and the environment was not progressive. The public service had the reputation of being a place where careers go to die slowly, where the excitement of youth is drained away and where there is stagnation and decay; in an undemocratic setting as Nigeria was at that time, the public service was a tool to rubber stamp authoritarian and corrupt military administrations. Young Accountants were more interested in the increasingly exciting private sector, particularly in the banks that were undergoing a boom at the time and where the pay and prospects were infinitely more attractive. However, not wanting to continue to sit idly by at home indefinitely, he took the suggestion serious and applied. In a few weeks he was called for a series of interviews which culminated in a job offer. As fate would have it, on the 4th of November 1985, Akin's civil service career started as an Accountant Grade 2 with the then Lagos State Waste Disposal Board at Ijora, at the age of just 22 years old and with a starting salary of a modest N324 per month.

With a staff strength of over 3000 staff of diverse cadres and most being casual staff and labourers, Akin had his work cut out for him. His duties included preparing salaries, wages and emoluments for all workers of the Waste Disposal Board. This was to be the beginning of an over 25-year journey as a public servant.

At this time, accounting work was extremely rudimentary, done manually on a worksheet called 'Kalamazoo', and having such a large number of casual staff, work was a great challenge. Also, by this time, the public service had several officers who had no university degree and most of his contemporaries in the office were so many years his senior in age. In fact, he was the youngest in his grade range and his deputy was nearly 60 years old. Nevertheless, he turned all obstacles into advantages, making the best use of all his past experiences and learning a great deal from his older colleagues at the office. He used what would have intimidated some and frustrated others, to be the very building blocks on which he would turn every experience, whether positive or negative, into a learning experience.

Working as it were, with so many older people also provided a great opportunity to also understand and manoeuver through the etiquette and demands of the public service. Being the most senior in rank and qualifications, yet youngest in age, one can also be at a disadvantage, but his attitude of eagerly wanting to serve and improve on what he found on ground, made those he worked with inspired to put their best foot forward too. He seized the initiative and made the best use of his opportunity to innovate and improve and was surprised that the public service allowed the changes he proposed. At a very early stage in his career, he took the decision first of all not to blend in and lose himself and his ideals, beliefs, style, presentation and principles, even with his dress code and idealism. Secondly, he never lost his drive to improve, he was allowed to make an impact and this energized and inspired both himself and all others around him. So he had an early opportunity to succeed and he eagerly applied himself to making an impact and sustaining the pace with which he started.

Never one to rest on his laurels, it soon became clear to Akin that there was a limit to which he would get to with his bachelor degree in Accounting and this would never be enough to be successful. It was obvious to him that in the dynamic world of Accounting and Finance, which at the time, with the advent of Computer Technology, was becoming more challenging as the years went by; he quickly realized that he would have to go further in his education to keep abreast with the developments. Not to mention that the older one got, the harder it would be to return to the classroom. Early in his career, he had promised himself that he would do whatever he needed to do academically to be successful as an Accountant. The time had come for him to move forward with his academic plans. One year after he started as Accountant Grade 2 in the Lagos State Waste Disposal Board, Akin went ahead and registered for both his ICAN certification and his Master's degree programme at the University of Lagos. It was time for some self improvement and being a great believer in striking while the iron is hot, Akin set himself a timeline to achieve his next academic hurdles before too much time went by to ruin his resolve.

> *"In order that people may be happy in their work, these three things are needed: they must be fit for it; they*

must not do too much of it; and they must have a sense of success in it – not a doubtful sense, such as needs some testimony of other people for its confirmation, but a sure sense, or rather knowledge, that so much work has been done well, and fruitfully done, whatever the world may say or think about it."

– *John Ruskin.*

CHAPTER FIVE

Multi-tasking Thrives!

"Do not pray for easy lives, pray to be stronger men. Do not pray for tasks equal to your powers; pray for powers equal to your tasks. Then the doing of your work shall be no miracle, but you shall be a miracle. Everyday you shall wonder at yourself, at the richness of life which has come to you by the grace of God."

— *Phillip Brooks.*

Akin decided in 1986 to take the concept of multi-tasking to a whole new level, some would say an impossible level, to complete and attain his ICAN professional certification and Master's degree in under two years. To take on these two arduous tasks and still work full time as well, showed the determination he had to aggressively move his life ever forward, not being scared of the challenges or the volume of work that he would inevitably have to put in. Some people would have opted for doing these two very demanding courses consecutively, especially taking into account that a full time job was demanding enough, but Akin put himself on a timetable and chose to run them concurrently. He knew it would take everything he had to accomplish this feat so he threw himself into it wholeheartedly.

Having always been someone who thrives on overcoming obstacles, Akin buckled down to the immense workload, putting all social activities on hold and running from one taskmaster to another. He would start the day at work and at the close of work, would make his way to the University of Lagos for his lectures and course work for his Master's programme. This was his routine from Monday to Friday. Then on the weekends, he would attend his classes for his ICAN certification. The workload was punishing, but having set himself this challenge, he refused to be daunted and capitulate; instead he focused unrelentingly on achieving his goal.

The year passed slowly, his workload at work grew and required him to be more efficient in spite of the lack of computerization; at the University, lectures were tedious, course work was heavy and he also had tutorials and assignments to complete. As if this was not enough, he had to totally devote his weekends to his ICAN certification lectures. It was a herculean effort; but dropping out was not an option he would consider. Soon

Multi-Tasking Thrives!

enough the exams for both drew close and Akin moved the preparations for his exams into high gear.

Then without warning another tragedy struck suddenly throwing everything he had worked for into a tailspin; a fraud perpetrated by some workers at the office led to the entire department being arrested and detained at the Police Station while detectives did their investigations. This happened the weekend before his first semester Master's exams. On the morning of the exams, Akin was released after being cleared of any wrongdoing. He immediately rushed to the University of Lagos to sit his exams, but on getting there, he arrived too late to enter the exam hall. He had missed his first semester exams and this was to set him back several months. At this point, he could have thrown in the towel and given up, but he remembered when his father passed on after his A' Levels; that would have been a good time to throw in the towel too. The remembrance of that victory reminded him that he had the capacity to turn this set back around, that he had the obligation to meet the goals he set for himself. He decided to put the whole incident behind him and remain focused on his timeline to complete both courses, in spite of the fact that his timing might be affected by several months.

By the end of 1987, Akin sat for and passed his ICAN certification exams, becoming a Chartered Accountant at 24 years old. By 1988, he also sat for and completed his Master's degree programme at the University of Lagos earning for himself a Master of Science degree just before his 25th birthday, and all the while, working as an Accountant for the Lagos State Waste Disposal Board. It was a feat that seemed like a pipe dream, but it had been accomplished in grand style.

Akin learnt some major lessons during his multi-tasking years; he learnt that he was stronger than he thought he was and could push himself really hard if he needed to. He learnt that keeping one's focus was the only way to successfully complete any task one sets for oneself; he learnt that obstacles always come up to derail any task, but success comes from not giving in to the obstacles. He learnt that whatever one wanted was possible, but only with hardwork, focus and dedication. He also learnt that multi-tasking should be used as a tool to move one rapidly in the direction of one's dreams and that human beings have the capacity to achieve as much as they go after. He learnt that multi-tasking is something that should be learnt as early as possible so as to become a character trait and not viewed as a burden. He realized that every child must be taught how to multi-task because the story of life is not played on straight lines; life is lived in multiple layers and on parallel lines; once one can tackle many things at once at an early stage, in one's latter years, multiple challenges are easier to address simultaneously.

It had been two long, grueling, hard years, but they had been well worth the effort.

"Every trouble is an opportunity to win the grace of strength. Whatever else trouble is in the world for; it is here for this good purpose – to develop strength. For a trouble is a moral and spiritual task. It is something which is hard to do. And it is in the spiritual world as in the physical; strength is increased by encounter with the difficult. A world without any trouble in it would be, to people of our kind, a place of spiritual enervation and moral laziness. Fortunately, everyday is crowded with care. Everyday to everyone of us brings its questions, its worries and its tasks, brings its sufficiency of trouble. Thus we get our daily spiritual exercise. Everyday we are blessed with new opportunities for the development of strength of soul."

– George Hodges.

CHAPTER SIX

The Local Government Years: Grassroots and Loving It

"Reach high, for stars lie hidden in your soul. Dream deep, for every dream precedes the goal."

– *Pamela Vaull Starr.*

In 1988, Lagos State was growing and developing faster than it had anticipated; there was a need for management positions to be filled by young, qualified and hardworking people and the Lagos State Local Government Service Commission was recruiting, looking for qualified people within the service to move up. Having his ICAN under his belt and his Master's months away, Akin was offered a Grade level 10 job as a Senior Accountant, while he was still on Grade level 8, at the

Waste Disposal Board. Such a jump would have been unheard of, but for his qualifications. Based on merit and his new certification alone, he had become eligible for Grade level 10. Akin took the opportunity and went for it.

The promotion came with a move to the beautiful Badagry town; it would mean a move away from family again, but this time, not too far away. Badagry was great in many ways; it represented a new birth; life in a beautiful, serene and historic town, a world away from the hustle and bustle of Metropolitan Lagos to the grassroots, the very base on which government rests and a double promotion, a great movement in Akin's career. As the Assistant Treasurer to the Badagry Local Government, his duties and responsibilities also doubled. He oversaw all the expenditure and revenue generation of the Local Government and in addition, had to assist the Treasurer immensely in his work.

Living in Badagry, Akin saw a different side to life from what he was used to. The one-on-one interaction with others at the Local Government level opened his eyes to the importance of serving selflessly and the importance of making an impact. The grassroots need a huge investment in time, infrastructure and training yet there is little recompense for one's labours here and these are the very pillars that the larger government is based on; if one has to get it right at the top, one must first make it right at the grassroots. He saw that the grassroots are largely ignored and that little if any development in either infrastructure or capacity building goes on at that level, yet the grassroots is what supports the entire superstructure of government; the foundation must be put right and strengthened for real progress to show. He set about improving and innovating, remembering his success in getting changes made to the way things were always done and making service his focus.

Akin learnt a lot from his Badagry years; he learnt to love and appreciate the simplicity of suburban Lagos, he learnt to value the 'no frills' and simple interaction with staff at the Badagry Local Government Office, he learnt how to serve and not count the cost or expect anything in return and he saw the quiet dignity and silent diligence of those who work at this level of governance. Badagry prepared him for the many years of working at this grassroots level. Being in and among the community on a daily basis, living with the authenticity and grace of the citizens of Badagry, learning their idiosyncrasies and studying the best ways to make a difference at this level consumed Akin during these years; he took the time to develop a listening ear, seeing eyes and helping hands. Without realizing the importance of his Badagry experience, Akin would make these years the template on which to build his Local Government system of service. After three years of living and working at Badagry, the time came to move on.

Akin was sent to Shomolu Local Government as Auditor. This too brought its own challenges. Shomolu is miles away from Badagry, not just in geographical distance, but also in the attitude of the people. Residents of Badagry are relaxed and serene; Shomolu residents are energetic, loud and frenetic. As a result of its nearness to the seat of Government in Ikeja, not to mention its long history of being one of the stalwarts in the Local Government hierarchy, Shomolu brought its own special set of challenges. Shomolu is not suburban bliss like Badagry; it is well within the Lagos metropolis and is home to several business concerns, markets, institutions and other inner city peculiarities. Shomolu has major infrastructure needs and space constraints. Akin had his work cut out for him here.

Before long, Akin packed his bags again to Alimosho Local Government as the Council Treasurer. Alimosho is one of the most densely settled Local Government areas in the State with the highest population and this often means being sympathetic to various shades of opinion and accommodating a large number of needs. Again, as with all his other postings, Akin found Alimosho to be interesting, because it is a great melting pot of many of the various tribes in Nigeria and is a great trading hub. It borders with Ogun State and is home to a great many factories and manufacturing concerns. Alimosho was also challenging; areas of great economic activity in Lagos State are generally chaotic; one needs to be strong, yet fair. Akin enjoyed the challenges of Alimosho and being a disciplined person, he made sure the Council ran in a regimented way.

A second move back to Shomolu Local Government, this time as Council Treasurer and later on to Mushin Local Government, again as Council Treasurer had Akin moving around the State and leaving his mark everywhere he went.

Mushin Local Government is uniquely different from almost all others; Mushin is politically speaking, a hot bed party faithful. Strong political roots run deep and the residents are extremely aware of their unique place in the political map of the State. Citizens of Mushin are very vocal and always demand a high level of service. Their political pedigree means they are critical, extremely politically aware and serve as a rallying point for grassroots politics. To survive in Mushin takes patience, innovation, intelligence and hardwork, but it pays great dividends because getting it right in Mushin means one can succeed in any other Local Government Area of the State.

In totality, Akin served in the Local Government Service for 10 years, from 1988-1998. It is pertinent here to point out that almost all Local Government Areas of Lagos State is home to millions of residents; Lagos Local Government Areas having the kind of population figures of some entire countries. There are real challenges and tremendous responsibilities for Public servants who work in these areas. There are high expectations and serious demands for excellence in serving in Lagos State. One of the distinguishing characteristics of the State is that historically speaking, Lagos had always been the trend setter and treasure base of the colonial government and positioned itself early in its existence as the economic power house of the nation.

Presently as the commercial nerve centre and former capital city of the most populous nation in Africa, Lagos has perhaps the highest number of educated people anywhere on the continent and the most vibrant middle class. This creates an immense amount of pressure on all tiers of governance, especially local and state Public servants.

Also, the real meaning of governance can be found at the Local Government level; without gainsaying, the closest government to the people; the best institution one can find to serve selflessly and be deeply satisfied that one has made a difference. As the record will show later, the gains of his Local Government Service have been deeply responsible for the successful tenure of Akin as the Accountant-General of Lagos State. In Akin's words, *"…if you work successfully at Local Government level and you are able to make a difference, there is nowhere else you cannot work successfully."*

CHAPTER SEVEN

The Hubert Humphrey Scholar Awakens

"Youth is past when the sensation of adventure is ended, when instead of boundless expectation and of curiosity that penetrates into all the corners of existence, a man is content to take things as they are, when eagerness gives way to complacency and questioning to the cynicism of experience. The man devoid of curiosity is the man who in the end attains to nothing."

— *The Living Age.*

After ten years of serving Lagos State at the grassroots level of governance, Akin was offered a rare opportunity. Once again, something great was about to unfold in his life that would change him forever. In August 1998, through the Hubert H. Humphrey

Fellowship Programme, the American Fulbright Scholarship Programme at Boston University, Massachusetts would turn his world upside down. Once again, he would leave home and family and embark on another voyage of discovery.

The Hubert Horatio Humphrey Fellowship Programme was established by the American Congress in 1978 in honour of the late Senator and Vice President, Senator Hubert Horatio Humphrey. Hubert Humphrey, the son of a pharmacist, was born in Wallace, South Dakota on 27th May, 1911. Educated at the University of Minnesota, Humphrey was unfortunately forced to abandon his studies when his father's business collapsed in 1932. After helping his father to resurrect the family business, Humphrey returned to university and finally graduated in 1939. Humphrey was an active member of the Democratic Party and worked as Campaign Manager for Franklin Delano Roosevelt, the longest serving American President (four Presidential terms) in Minnesota during the 1944 presidential election. The following year, Humphrey was elected mayor of Minneapolis. Perhaps because of his experience with lean times, he always had a heart for the struggling masses. As such he became a strong supporter of civil rights, and a leading member of the American Democratic Action pressure group. In the 1948 Democratic National Convention, Humphrey supported Harry S. Truman and his Fair Deal proposals, which included legislation on civil rights, fair employment practices and opposition to lynching. When

Truman won the Democratic Party nomination, Southern Democrats formed the States' Rights Democratic Party (Dixiecrats) and Storm Thurmond was chosen as its presidential candidate.

Humphrey was elected to the Senate in 1948. Over the next fifteen years he was in close association with many progressive causes including the formation of a Peace Corps, the creation of a Food for Peace programme and legislation favouring trade unions, African Americans and the unemployed. It may seem to us in these times that these are programmes that should be part of any developed country's strategy to be seen as a fair society at home and a relevant player on the world stage, but we must bear in mind that these were revolutionary ideas in their day and even today are laudable to say the least. It is also pertinent to note here that the Peace Corps helped a lot with reconstruction and morale boosting during and after the Nigerian Civil War in the 1970's, as they did and continue to do with other countries around the world.

During the period known as McCarthyism (1950-1954), members of the Republican Party and conservative members of the Democratic Party, accused Humphrey of being "soft on Communism". However, Humphrey had always fought Communist Party influence in progressive organizations such as the American Democratic Action. Humphrey was defeated by John F. Kennedy in his attempt to become the Democratic Party's presidential candidate in 1960. He also failed in 1964, but the victor,

Lyndon Baines Johnson, made an excellent choice in selecting him as his Vice President and he was able to influence the decision to introduce the Voting Rights Act (1965) and the Immigration Act (1965).

In 1968 Humphrey was chosen as the party's presidential candidate against Richard Nixon of the Republican Party. With progressive forces in the country unhappy with Humphrey's support of the Vietnam War, (seen as a huge mistake) and with George Wallace collecting over 9 million votes in the South, it was no surprise when he failed to win the election. Nixon won 31,770,237 votes against 31,270,533 for Humphrey, a very narrow win for Nixon. Humphrey subsequently went into education and took on a position at the University of Minnesota. After working as Professor of Public Affairs at the University of Minnesota for two years, Humphrey was once again elected to the Senate in 1970 and served well for several years before his untimely death caused by cancer of the bladder on 13th January, 1978.

In the spirit of a world leader concerned with the struggle of suffering masses and fostering international understanding, the objective therefore of the program is twofold: first, to permit mid-career professionals from Africa, Asia, Central and South America, Central and Eastern Europe to gain expertise in their fields as they have evolved in the United States; and second, to allow U.S. citizens in the business, government, and academic communities to profit from the knowledge and perspectives of professional counterparts in other countries and to establish lasting ties with them. This is because the qualities that most stand out in Hubert Humphrey's life are selfless service, equality, diligence, excellence, integrity and humility. He had a most compelling love for his fellow human being, not minding skin colour, creed or political persuasion. Perhaps this is why Hubert Humphrey Scholars and Fellows, in identifying with the life and achievements of this great man, always make an impact when they return from their year of study. They seem to be hugely impacted by his love of service with the utmost humility and incredible sacrifice, not in a sanctimonious and self aggrandizing manner, but in a humble, self effacing and quiet way.

As part of the Fulbright International Educational Exchange activities, the Humphrey Fellowship Programme is funded through the United States Department of State and administered nationally by the Institute of International Education. Boston University has supported the programme since its inception and has hosted 433 Humphrey Fellows from 118 countries to date. Under the personal guidance of faculty mentors and program coordinators, Fellows engage in individualized programmes of graduate-level coursework, independent research, special seminars, and colloquia at the University, and in activities related to their professional fields in government agencies, private organizations, and corporations. Akin was selected to become a Fellow of one of the most prestigious Alumni's, to further enhance his education and help make an impact on his return to

Lagos State, which by this time was the commercial force on the continent.

Boston was a long way from home in more ways than one, not to mention that it is the very antithesis of Lagos. Boston gets brutally cold, Lagos is always a comfortable summer; it is an ultra modern, highly developed, sophisticatedand cerebral city, Lagos is nowhere near in terms of infrastructure, culture and ambience; Boston is a uniquely historic city, deeply rooted in American tradition, yet quite cosmopolitan and some might say quite contemporary, Lagos is largely a colonial creation, swallowed by the euphoria of Independence, inspired by the success stories of the big players in the Western Hemisphere, handicapped by its meager geographical boundaries, burdened by its gargantuan and diverse population and working hard to carve out an authentic, yet all inclusive identity. Yet for all the differences, there are uncanny similarities; Bostonians are unapologetically politically savvy, sometimes even ahead of Washingtonians, with an almost arrogant attitude of their political antecedence; Lagosians altruistically and stubbornly refuse to be bullied by Abuja, politically play the 'devil's advocate' and may lack a concise political culture, but are the most sophisticated state, most discerning and indeed the most mature electorate of the country. The juxtaposition of both cities is interesting on several levels; very different yet very similar. The opportunity to bring back a bit of the Boston experience was extremely compelling for Akin. So once again he packed his bags and headed for Boston and a fortuitous scholarship that would reinvent him, reinvigorate his focus and redefine his life.

> *"Last night, Dr. Martin Luther King, Jr., died a martyr's death. His death snatched from American life something rare and precious; the living reminder that one man can make a difference - that one man, by the force of his character, the depth of his convictions, and the eloquence of his voice - can alter the course of history. What a testimonial to individualism, what a testimonial to dignity and to human purpose - for Martin Luther King had the courage to challenge the intolerance, the injustice, inadequacies and inequities of the society in which he lived - a nation that he loved - a nation of which he was a citizen - and a nation for which he prayed and worked."*
>
> *– Hubert Humphrey, speech at a meeting of the National Alliance of Businessmen at Long Island the day after the assassination of Martin Luther King. (5th April, 1968).*

CHAPTER EIGHT

Resolving to Innovate, Ready to Serve

"Serving freely without concealed intent adds a little more in the realm of goodness and kindness."

– Akin Ambode.

The Hubert Humphrey year at Boston came to an end in 1999 and Akin was, by this time, a changed man in more ways than one. For one thing, the program seeks to transform the mindset of the man, making the man see himself as a well oiled cog in a well oiled machine, just one of many excellent working parts. This tends to create and feed a team spirit as opposed to a 'lone ranger' or 'superman' spirit. He creates a team and this team shares the burden, responsibility, work and sacrifices and also enjoys the results, accomplishments and accolades which come from collective excellence.

Secondly, the programme seeks to transform the man himself; anything short of personal excellence is not enough. Everyone must bring their best foot forward; it is not a place for mediocrity or just being barely there. The individual excellence of each team member creates conditions where diligence, integrity, creativity, innovation and service thrive. The very presence of these qualities brings about the transformation of the man.

Thirdly, the programme seeks to transform the workplace into which the man returns. Since the transformed man returns with higher standards across the board, co-workers see a vastly different man with a new work ethic and a new resolve to serve selflessly, come back to their fold with a renewed vigor and a new and positive attitude to everything. This rubs off on others and raises their former level of service. Being around a Hubert Humphrey scholar can be infectious, albeit in a good way.

Fourthly, the programme seeks to transform the society into which the man returns. By returning a renewed man with a Hubert Humphrey pedigree, it goes without saying that such a man will not rest until he affects every level on which he operates. Transforming the society is the key to success that unlocks even greater success. The hallmark of a Humphrey man is to bring the change he has experienced back into his workplace, society, country and seek to transform it into the best version of itself. The Humphrey man is consumed with a deep desire to affect everything around him to the degree that only the best becomes the standard.

The beauty of the programme is based on several observations that have fine tuned the way the programme works. The types of university programmes arranged for Humphrey Fellows depart from a traditional discipline-oriented focus and have a problem-solving and experience-sharing emphasis. The programmes are not degree-related or aimed at providing scholarly preparation or basic training in a field. The objective is to provide Humphrey Fellows and scholars with an overall experience that broadens their perspectives, enhances their capability to assume greater career responsibilities, create in them a strong empathy for the less privileged in their societies and provides opportunities to establish useful professional contacts. To accomplish these objectives, programmes are designed to include various combinations of course work, independent projects, internships, consultations with U.S. faculty experts, field trips, and special seminars. Under the guidance of a designated faculty advisor or 'coordinator', Fellows and scholars plan programmes that best suit their individual career development needs. However to reiterate, selfless service to society, being a major goal is one area that is not ignored.

Akin's Boston experience did all these and more. The period made him resolve to take service to a higher level than before; it re-engineered his entire educational experience, the exposure to the American way of doing things transformed his former ways and expanded the 'can-do' attitude he had. It solidified his belief that there was nothing that was unattainable when one serves selflessly and from the heart. It further enriched his social capital base; with so many International alumni added to his contacts, all his perceived boundaries came crashing down. With the disappearance of his boundaries, Akin became the mantra of the Hubert Humphrey Fellow, **"...one person can make a difference and that person can be you..."**

To really grasp the impact of the training one only has to see the impressive achievements of those touched by the programme, for they are all over the world, in 157 countries, on all continents, with 44 campuses, 204 Fellows and 4, 492 Alumni of which 109 (and counting) are Nigerians.

The impact of these alumni on the world is impressive. Fellows have gone on to become Presidents, Governors, Members of Parliament, leading human-rights Activists, Supreme Court Justices, Ambassadors and Financial Experts, to name just a few. Years after completing the fellowship, these accomplished alumni reported that they were still energized and inspired by their experience abroad. *"If someone is dedicated and committed, I can't see how they can come out of the fellowship without changing their community,"* says Geraldine Chin, a Cameroonian women's-rights activist who completed her fellowship at an American University in 2006. *"It is a life-changing programme."*

CHAPTER NINE

The State Service

"We will never bring disgrace to this our nation by any act of dishonesty or cowardice, nor ever desert our suffering comrades in the ranks. We will fight for the ideals of the nation both alone and with others. We will revere and respect our nation's laws, and do our best to incite a like respect and reverence in those above us who are prone to annul and set them at naught. We will strive unceasingly to quicken the public's sense of civic duty. Thus in all these ways we will transmit this nation not only not less but greater, better, and more beautiful than it was transmitted to us."

– James Russell Lowell.

If ever there was a time Akin was excited about his potentialities and abilities, it was when he returned from Boston, back to Lagos State and Public Service. He returned fully persuaded that he could make the difference between excellence and mediocrity and this he resolved to practise for the rest of his career and his life. Such was the impact of Boston; the Hubert Humphrey scholar never remains the same. He knew that he would never again settle for anything average; that wherever he found himself, he would make a difference in his work, his attitude, his ways and manners, his people and his community.

Akin returned to Lagos in November 1999 and he quickly set about bringing his ideas and plans into something concrete that would quickly begin to yield the results he longed for and justify the time, money and energy expended. On his return, he was still technically in the Local Government Service and had been recently deployed to Ajeromi/Ifelodun Local Government Area, then regarded as the most lucrative of all Local Government postings. At a meeting in Alausa, Akin expressed his desire to leave the Local Government Service and move to the State Public Service to the then Head of Service, Mr. Rafiu Tinubu. Seeing he had the credentials, the passion and the drive, the Head of Service gave his blessing and Akin moved to the State Service. His other colleagues were shocked at his desire to leave the Local Government Service at a time when he was right at the peak of the Local Government Service and when he was deployed to the most lucrative of all the Local Governments; they felt he was leaving a place that was secure and offered great benefits for one that was unsure and unchartered, but this kind of decision is vintage Akin; getting comfortable and not having challenges is unappealing and unacceptable to him. His style is to constantly look for challenges, solve problems, accomplish goals and continually set new targets; settling for comfortable certainty is an anathema.

His first assignment was as the Assistant Director of the Office of the Auditor General for Local Governments. This assignment lasted only three months, in February 2000, he became Acting Auditor General for Local Governments when the then Auditor General statutorily retired. This gave him the opportunity to put into practise his past experiences and his Hubert Humphrey year at Boston. In charge of over 250 staff and still rather young, Akin swung into action in his capacity as Acting Auditor General, a post he held for eighteen months until the then Governor of Lagos State was personally convinced that he was the right man for the job. The Lagos State House of Assembly confirmed his appointment by an Act of Parliament towards the end of 2001, when he formally became the Auditor General of Local Governments for Lagos State, at the age of just thirty seven years old.

This position required amongst other things, the oversight of all financial activities of all Local Governments Councils within Lagos State. He functioned in this capacity till January 2005, when he was redeployed to the main Public Service as the Permanent Secretary, Ministry of Finance. This was based solely on his record of service, assessments and dedication in his assignments. He was adjudged the most competent person to hold this position; a position that he breathed new life and vigor into, reworking the terms of reference, raising the bar in terms of service delivery, raising the standards in terms of staff morale and capacity building, redeveloping and retooling the office environment to function as a modern and efficient workplace, fine tuning the entire Ministry to function as a goal achieving and target driven entity.

In February 2006, Akin was to move still higher; this time as the Permanent Secretary and Accountant General for Lagos State. In this position, he was in charge of all the financial activities of the State and directly responsible for over 1,400 Accountants in the State Service. In the last nine years as the Permanent Secretary, Ministry of Finance, he recognized the need for the creation of a State Treasury Office, a leap forward in providing financial efficiency. Ever the innovator, he sought and obtained the go-ahead for this new addition to the Ministry of Finance.

The creation of the State Treasury Office (or STO as it is fondly called by its staff) has revolutionized the way and manner in which the finances of Lagos State is raised, budgeted, managed, planned and spent. The creation of the STO was a major victory; it has modernized the cumbersome work of administering the finances of the State to be in line with best practices and world standards, as well as helping the administration of Lagos State to become a key player financially in the country, the ECOWAS sub-Region and the Continent.

Akin has worked extensively on reforming the tax laws to be in line with new internationally accepted best practices. His vast input in reforming tax laws led to Lagos State becoming a model for all the other States and even for the Federal Government, to which he lent a lot of his expertise and experience during the conception and formulation of a new tax regime, a very bold and courageous step that other states are yet to emulate. During his time at the STO, Lagos State has become the first State in the Nigerian Federation to convert from the cumbersome and antiquated paper based systems to the more modern, internationally practiced e-based systems. Not to mention that this new e-based system has been shown to vastly cut down the incidence of corruption in the collection of taxes. A unique synergy between the Lagos State Government and the Banking industry makes the whole system work efficiently and effectively for the benefit of all concerned, especially for the citizens of the State who enjoy the benefits and dividends of these innovations. In a popular business newspaper, Business Day, of Tuesday 2nd July, 2013, it was reported that Fiscal Management in Lagos State had surpassed that of the Federal Government and internally generated revenue from taxes has touched the 75% mark in stark contrast to the Federal Governments' 20%. Also, the paper further stated that Lagos State makes up to 20% of total Nigerian GDP and 40% of non oil GDP. All these gains from the smallest state geographically (that is in terms of size) showing that Lagos State which is without any of the rich mineral resources that other states' have in abundance can think outside the box and create wealth using what little it has and building on its commercial base. These great strides are particularly noted to have happened in the last six years (2006-2012) during which Akin headed the STO.

As a committed member of the Institute of Chartered Accountants of Nigeria, he chalked up several accomplishments and within the state chapter of that body, has empowered several Accountants to be better equipped educationally for the challenges they face at work. This he achieved by creating an enabling environment; emphasizing diligence, creating training programmes, encouraging continuous certification and insisting on excellence.

He held his position as Permanent Secretary, State Treasury Office, Ministry of Finance up till his retirement from the State Public Service in August 2012; a period of which is known for a renaissance of sorts financially in Lagos State.

In all those years, Akin proved in different formats, in attitude, in productivity, in actions and in speech all the tenets of a Humphrey Fellow; everything about public leadership and selfless service comes through in his actions, his utterances, his attitudes, his efforts and his results. He counts his last thirteen years as being his most productive and most impactful having been able to touch the lives of so many, ignite the confidence of majority of those he has worked with and bring out the best of most of those he has come across.

In the twenty seven years that Akin served Lagos State from the early days of Ijora at the Waste Disposal Board to the hallowed chambers of the State Treasury Office of the Ministry of Finance, one can hardly perceive him as your typical Public Servant; he is not your run-of-the-mill, self absorbed bureaucrat, he is the very antithesis of what the Public Service has come to mean. He started twenty seven years ago refusing to get into the well known mould and decided instead to chart a totally different course for his service years. Having set his sights on attaining the highest standards of selfless service, he diligently steered the course of his career, ensuring that he left nothing undone and no challenge unanswered. It was twenty seven years of dedication, vision, service and diligence to the glory of God and to the service of the great Lagos State and its good citizens and there are no regrets. It had been twenty seven wonderful years.

> *"All human beings have failings; all human beings have needs, and temptations and stresses. Men and women who live together through long years get to know one another's failings; but they also come to know what is worthy of respect and admiration in those they live with and in themselves. If at the end, one can*

say, 'this man used to the limit the powers that God granted him; he was worthy of love and respect and of the sacrifices of many people, made in order that he might achieve what he deemed to be his task,' then that life has been lived well and there are no regrets."

– Eleanor Roosevelt.

CHAPTER TEN

Making a Difference, the Reluctant Role Model

"Treat people as if they are what they ought to be and you help them to become what they are capable of being."

– *Johann Wolfgang Von Goethe*

How surprisingly refreshing it is to find a man who has done so much, surmounted so many obstacles, touched so many lives, changed so many ways and inspired so many people, yet be so unwilling to take the credit and brand his colleagues and subordinates with the indelible mark of his identity. Akin remains to many an enigma, they struggle to understand and put him into a definite cubbyhole. He refuses to see himself as a role model, yet to many he is just that. He refuses to see himself as a boss, preferring instead to be a co-worker. He refuses to see himself as the leader, preferring instead to be a member of the team.

Mentoring for him is pointing one in the direction of their own dreams, not supplanting their dreams for his; for Akin, it is not enough that he becomes the best version of himself, but that he helps others become the best version of themselves too. When questioned about mentoring and being a role model for others he said,

> *"...sometimes I am confronted with the subject of mentoring and I am asked who my mentor is. Somehow I cannot place appropriate answers to some of these questions. Why? Because everyday, I am also confronted by situations which give one the opportunity to search for true leaders and even though they abound everywhere and a lot of us have the innate capacity to make a positive difference, we are never recorded as mentors, champions or true leaders. At different points in our lives, we have had relationships; a teacher, a boss, an employer, a friend, a parent who has greatly changed the way we looked at life and the world. Someone who inspired us and motivated us, someone who taught us to set goals and instilled the confidence and spirit to achieve them, someone who had high standards and truly stood for something; such a person is the real mentor we all need to find. I have found true leaders through such observations in the course of my career...they help you build your art of selfless service, but it is important too that you carve out for yourself an identity authentically your own, that you don't*

monkey another person's life so slavishly as to lose your own..."

Intrigued by his refusal to reel off his accomplishments and detail his large list of beneficiaries and achievements, yet knowing that it is impossible to have a balanced account of his service without the input of others, it is imperative that one seeks the opinions of those who spent time working with Akin. As such it became necessary to speak with staff of the State Treasury Office, his very last assignment. This brought a further layer of insight into the man, Akinwunmi Ambode. Below is a summary of what some former staff members had to say.

MRS. YEMISI ADAMS

I am a Grade level 12 Officer with the State Treasury Office in Operations Department. I was posted to this department six years ago. To me, he is a role model; he is a leader not a boss. A boss wants you to do things the way he says, there is no input coming from anyone, but for a leader, he will table the problem and some solutions, he will ask for opinions and feedback before taking decisions and will carry everyone along. He is someone I can emulate because he operates an open door policy; no matter your rank or level, you are free to walk in here and discuss with him, whether official or private matters. With the little encounter I have had with him so far, if others could try to copy his lifestyle, the civil service will be a place that everyone will like to work because once a person has an open door policy; you will not be scared or reluctant to bring in your own ideas towards efficient service delivery.

With what I have seen before I got here, there is most times a disconnect, a gap, because between Mr. Akin's level and mine, there is a difference and without being someone who is approachable, the relationship will not be so cordial, no one will want to come near, talk less of hearing your own opinion. He carries us along and makes us work independently. He wants our input to be visible, efficient, effective and selfless. Especially for senior civil servants, if you don't carry your subordinates along, if you have a goal, that goal may not be achieved. In some offices there are forceful bosses and it is when they are around that work goes on with people doing eye service, but because of Mr. Akin's style, work here goes on whether he is here or not, even after others have closed, so that we achieve our set goals.

There are a lot of things that I have learnt from him which I practise now and I pray that if I ever get to his level, I will continue to put all these things into practice. Some of these things are first, his open door policy, secondly, his habit of commending all staff, thirdly, the way he motivates us to reach and even surpass targets. He finds it easy to encourage us and this makes us work longer hours than others. Most days our colleagues in other ministries close by 4:00pm, while we are here till 8:00pm. Not because we get any over time, because we don't, but because of the work environment here and the way Mr. Akin is. He leads by example, he is a real leader.

Even when you know you are wrong, he doesn't treat you badly, he still finds a way to encourage you to get the work done. Some bosses are quick to give queries and will tell you off easily, but with him it is totally different. He once picked me up when I was stranded on my way to the office. How many bosses will do that? Even at home, I have changed the way I relate with others, imbibing his style.

He likes things being done promptly; he doesn't like people waiting so long to be attended to. He believes in time management, as long as you are in the office, he wants the work to get done efficiently and effectively.

Personally, it is because I came here that I got my professional degree; the first time I got here, we had a meeting with Mr. Akin and he challenged us all to be more professional, to grow and be better Accountants. That was when I made up my mind to go ahead and do my ICAN. He also supported me when I wanted to travel and encouraged me to think bigger. He doesn't like bragging about what he does, he does things very quietly. He helps whoever comes across him, not minding tribe, sex or religion.

MISS. OLUWAKEMI TOSO-GBANGBA

I had the opportunity to work with Mr. Ambode for ten years; I actually first worked with him when I joined the State Service and everything I know now, I learnt from him. He is the kind of person who believes in people, he believes so much that everybody has the potential to do anything. He believes so much in multi-tasking; you cannot tell him that because you are not an Accountant you cannot do any Accounting; he is a real role model.

He encourages one to grow, he is a great team player; he listens to one about anything. I feel he is a workaholic; he believes in getting the job done. He is prim, proper and believes in perfection, he is a neat person and believes that the office environment must be conducive to work because we spend most of our time there. When you compare this place (the STO) with other offices, you may not want to work because of the way things are there, but here, there is the conducive atmosphere and the tools to work with. He doesn't believe you should wait for government to do everything, he feels you should get things done yourself. He constantly works towards perfection and wants to see everyone grow in their profession, he encourages us to do professional exams and improve ourselves and the way we think by reading all types of books.

He always has time to listen to whatever problems we have, whether official or personal. I sometimes wonder how he copes with all the demands on him. He is a good person; he has a good heart. Sometimes he can be hard on us, but he always says mindless effort is not rewarded, but hardwork and good results are. I have never seen him as a tribalistic person or a chauvinist; he doesn't see people in that sort of light, for him, anyone can do well.

He taught me to believe in myself; to not see problems, but search for solutions. I can say I definitely work better, more efficiently and effectively because of all the things I have picked up from him. He encouraged me to do external exams and get all my certification.

MR. HAKEEM ALIMI

I have worked with Mr. Ambode for over six years now and his style is not the usual civil service style, it is a good mix of public/private sector style. Even when he is not present, we work as if he is around; he has trained us to work well with or without supervision. I have worked in the private sector, in multinationals as well as smaller companies and I can say his style is quite like what you have in such companies. He doesn't like red tape or bureaucracy, he believes we must deliver, not waste time in treating an issue. He has trained us not to waste time because as he says, you never know the urgency of something awaiting your attention.

He is an equal opportunity person, he doesn't believe in favouring women over men or men over women. He is a multi-tasker, the demand on his time is so great, but he always attends to every issue. He is somebody that one should emulate; I am a Muslim and he is a Christian, yet I have never felt there is any difference between us; he does not discriminate in any way. He is unique in terms of kindness, in terms of being professional; he is a wonderful person. He does love perfection and has a very high standard in all ramifications; you see it professionally, you see it in the way he dresses, you see it in the way he relates to his staff, you see it in everything he does. At our last Accountants conference I had the opportunity to sit beside one of the Facilitators briefly. He asked me if I knew the value of Mr. Ambode, if we really appreciate him at the STO; this is someone who is in private practice somewhere, he just knows him on a professional level. Mr. Ambode's reasoning on things is superb; if I call him a genius, I have not overstated the issue. I am very lucky to have worked with him. I have gained a lot in terms of confidence, I learnt from him to be very thorough, to do my work so well that I can stand by whatever I do. Another thing I have learnt from him is not to be biased, not to stereotype people, whether women or men, Christian or Muslim, Yoruba, or Igbo, or Hausa or whatever, to be ready to accommodate anyone regardless of differences. I have also decided to emulate him when it comes to my appearance; to always look clean, neat and professional, to project a confident image from head to toe, Monday to Sunday.

It is my opinion that one of the secrets to his success is his charity; his compassion and love for people. God has given him a huge capacity for empathy, to put himself in other peoples' shoes; he is a great helper and forgives wrongs so easily. Not many people have the heart to be charitable; it is a gift from God.

MRS. OLUMUYIWA OJELABI

I have worked with Mr. Ambode for just less than a year now. In all the places I worked previously, I think this place is the best by far. His style is not the usual civil service style at all, he is so different. He is very efficient and demands excellence always, but he is not so difficult that he doesn't understand that we have problems and limitations because our work usually dovetails with other ministries. He understands that he may not be able to rely on others outside this place, but when it comes to us at the State Treasury Office, the standard is very high and we do our best to keep that standard high. He always talks about being a better person in all things, he likes constant growth. It is not enough that you did well last week; you must do well this week and the next, not because you want a reward, but because it is the right thing to do.

He does not discriminate; he demands the same high standards whether you are a man or a woman. One thing that amazed me so much was this; there was a morning I was walking behind him on the corridor, he saw an empty bottle of coke lying around, he didn't call the cleaner and shout like some people might. Instead, he picked it up and took it to the pantry himself and continued to his office. He is a humble person; imagine the most senior officer here not thinking he is too good to do something so simple. He is an example to all.

Even when you are wrong about something he doesn't castigate you, he will just encourage you to be better; he is a kind person.

In some departments, you have to stand up if a senior officer enters your work space, but he doesn't like such formalities, he always tells us to just continue our work as if he is not there. He is very approachable; you can go to him over any issue and in spite of how busy he is, he will make time to see you.

MR. OSINUBI TAOFEEK OLALEKAN

I am a Grade level 12 Principal Administrative Officer with twelve years experience in the Public Service, of which I have spent two years here at the State Treasury Office, working under Mr. Ambode. He is not like others, he is not your typical Civil Servant, he does not work like a typical Civil Servant, but like someone in the private sector; he carries all the staff along, he is a motivator, he inspires you to be better everyday.

He has a listening ear; with him you have the confidence that if you have a problem, you can go to him for advice, and that advice will be confidential and good. He does not discriminate and has no biases, everyone can be better; everyone can do anything, whether you are a man or a woman. He is extremely efficient, extremely intelligent and he creates an atmosphere of order. You can see that the State Treasury Office is the best of all the departments. Yes, the Lagos

State Public Service is the best in the country and STO is the very best in the Lagos State Public Service.

Personally, since I started here, I love coming to work, this surprises me; because when you work in a place like this, your best comes to the fore, you feel you have made a difference and you are making an impact.

MR. TAIWO WAKEEL

I am a Principal Administrative Officer of twelve years with the Public Service. I have worked for just over a year with Mr. Ambode. He is a financial technocrat, a good leader and a financial expert. He is humble and easy to relate to. I have no fear in speaking with him. He always gives good advice. You can see that the State Treasury Office looks different from any other place in this facility, it looks just like a private sector office and we have everything we need here to be efficient and effective. This is how Mr. Ambode has made it so that we work here very well.

Personally, I think he is guided by God to move the STO forward. Being in charge of the finance of the State Government is the most difficult job in the State service. We have to work with all other ministries and departments and our work is much more than others.

If you work with Mr. Ambode you can be assured of two things: one, you will work very hard and two, you will close late. He makes us achieve set goals and targets and he has completely changed the way I used to work, because when you work with a hard worker, you will also have to work hard.

He is an equal opportunity man; there is no advantage for women over men or men over women, he believes everyone can do great things. He doesn't look at religion or sex or age or tribe, all he wants is for everyone to become excellent.

When I first came here, I was afraid of him and I would sometimes dodge him to avoid being near him. Then, he was always complaining about the state of cleanliness. But when I understood his style, that his standards are very high and once you can raise yours, you will have nothing to fear; then I stepped up the level of my work. Now, I go to see him whenever I need to because he has a listening ear and solves everyone's problems. Around the STO, we call him 'Baba Laanu'; he has great goodwill with all staff.

My exposure to him has made me a better person; I now enjoy learning about financial matters even though I am an Administrator. I know I can learn anything."

The foregoing comments are just a few of the many testimonials from those who have worked with Akin, all basically stating the same thing; that no matter where you are born or what the circumstances of your life are, it is possible to become the kind of person that can become a model for others to emulate. It is possible no matter the odds, to succeed and inspire others to do the same.

Here is a man that in spite of many odds, dug deep and found the courage and determination to be an agent of change and a selfless servant to his God, his country and his fellow man. Here is a man that others can call a mentor, even if he sees himself as just being the best he can be.

> *"A true leader sees his work as selfless service towards a higher purpose. A true leader should be judged by what he has not – ego, arrogance and self interest."*
>
> *– Akin Ambode.*

Former Head of Service, now Hon. Member of Lagos State House of Assembly with Mr. Akin Ambode

Senator Bola Ahmed Tinubu
Former Governor, Lagos State with Mr. Akin Ambode

Mrs Ifueko Omogui-Okauru
Former Chairman - FIRS with Mr. Akin Ambode at first ever National Tax Retreat, 2005

Alhaji Dankwambo
Former Accountant General of the Federation at FAAC meeting 2010 with Akin Ambode

Mr. Rotimi Oyekan
Accountants' Retreat 2010, surrounded by other Accountants in the State Public Service.

Federal Govt. College Warri, Old Students Association Cricket Club at Practice.

Mr. Akin Ambode

CHAPTER ELEVEN

A Man of Numbers

"The beauty of work depends upon the way we meet it, whether we arm ourselves each morning to attack it as an enemy that must be vanquished before night comes – or whether we open our eyes with the sunrise to welcome it as an approaching friend who will keep us delightful company and who will make us feel at evening that the day was well worth its fatigue.

– *Lucy Larcom.*

Where Law lost out, Accountancy won a great victory. Akin had initially wanted to be a man of letters; he had flirted severally with the thought of studying Law and had actually applied to study Law as his second choice course of study, but having done so well in his A' levels, he got in to study his first choice course,

Accountancy. Akin was always a man of numbers; he thrived in his chosen course and loving it so much gave him the impetus to keep going further in his profession. What many people do not know is that as an Accountant, he not only distinguished himself personally, but also did his utmost to make sure that the members of the profession, at least within the purview of the Public service, became the best they could possibly be.

Speaking with Mr. Sakirudeen Odusanya, a Deputy Director of Accounts in the Office of Environmental Services, Ministry of the Environment, Lagos State, one would find the progression of Akin's life of numbers most inspiring. In his own words:

> "It all dates back to 1991 when I first met Mr. Ambode at Shomolu. Then he was the Auditor for Shomolu Local Government Council. He was most helpful to me, once he met me and found out that I wanted to go further in the profession, he agreed to sign my ICAN form so that I could achieve my dream. I remember the quality of his work at the Local Government level; he was like a breath of fresh air, everything he did was of the highest quality. He encouraged all of us to always perform at the highest level no matter how mundane the task. He never condoned a half hearted work ethic, to work with him; one always had to do the very best. There was a time then when he went on pilgrimage to Jerusalem. While he was there, he was involved in an accident that kept him away from work for about three months. I found myself acting in his capacity for those months and even though he might not have been able

to come to the office, nothing went by him unnoticed or unattended. He supervised everything until he was well again to come physically to the office. While he was away, some people would report unfavourable things to him, but he is not one to discuss people, he abhors that kind of behaviour; any gossip, rumour, speculation or intrigue is unpalatable to him. He told me then to just work hard and be able to defend my work. He is only interested in issues and how to solve problems and surmount challenges. I really missed him when he was transferred away from there. Due to the fact that he really made an impression on me, I followed his progress everywhere he went and made sure I kept in touch with him throughout the years. At the State Government level, he left nothing the same, from the toilets to the corridors, the offices to the equipment, the staff of all cadres; he would challenge everyone all the time to step up the level of their work. Others saw what he was doing and the results he was getting and started changing things around them as well. That is how he is; he never leaves a place the way he finds it, especially if it is not performing to high standards."

So how did the world of Accountancy fare as a result of his passion for numbers? Mr. Odusanya, who is presently the Chairman of the Public Service State Chapter of the Institute of Chartered Accountants of Nigeria, was most helpful:

"Mr. Ambode was the brain behind the Public service chapter being registered and recognized. He made it possible for all Accountants in the Public service,

> including those in state agencies, to come under one umbrella body. Previously in Lagos State, there were only two public sector chapters, the Unilag chapter and the PHCN chapter. He realized the importance of all Accountants who work for the State, not to be excluded from the profession for lack of registration. This has really helped us in terms of recognition from the National body, in terms of available training, in terms of self esteem. Presently, we are even the most populous chapter and this gives us great joy and clout within our professional body. With his mentoring, one cannot remain ordinary. Presently, he is the Life Patron of our chapter; having him there in that capacity really helps us so much. He encourages us to become better Accountants and is a highly esteemed and respected member in the State chapter."

What lessons can we learn from this man so passionate about his profession? Mr. Odusanya, drawing from personal experience answered avidly;

> "Mr. Ambode is truly a mentor; he is my mentor. He wants perfection in the practicing of one's profession; to not do one's best is unacceptable to him. He taught us to treat issues as and when they arise as swiftly as possible, because he says time is too important to waste. He doesn't believe in one's desk overflowing with papers and files everywhere; to him, that is a sign that work is not getting done. He hates people being kept waiting; he hates people thinking they have to know someone to be attended to. He is so passionate about the profession that he paid for my induction and does so

> *much for many, many others, but you will not know because he does things without boasting about it. He wants all the Accountants in the Lagos State public service to be the best they can be and believes that that will make a big difference, because just like Lawyers, everyone needs an Accountant. We are stronger and better placed today because he cares."*

In his inimitable way, Akin elevates his beloved profession in a way only a Humphrey Fellow could and continues to do so still. He remains a man of numbers, in love with numbers and the diligent practice of same.

> *"The highest reward for man's toil is not what he gets for it but what he becomes by it."*
> – John Ruskin.

CHAPTER TWELVE

Still the Same Person

"Most of us can afford to take a lesson from the oyster. The extraordinary thing about the oyster is this; irritations get into its shell. He does not like them. He tries to get rid of them. But when he cannot get rid of them he settles down to make them one of the most beautiful things in the world. He uses the irritation to do the loveliest thing that an oyster ever has a chance to do. If there are irritations in our lives today, there is only one prescription: make a pearl. It may have to be a pearl of patience, but, anyhow, make a pearl. And it takes faith and love to do it."

– *Harry Emerson Fosdick.*

In spite of all the irritations, challenges, losses, failures, disappointments, draw backs and defeats that have peppered his life and times, Akin remains the same person he was when he first started out on his journey of life all those many years ago; wiser, stronger and better, yes of course, but essentially the same. He has had many irritations and like the oyster, he turned them into pearls. He has had many challenges; he turned them into hurdles and then jumped over them. He has had many losses; he made his peace and moved on. He has had many failures; he turned each one into a learning experience. He has had disappointments; he turned them into appointments with God and made sense out of them. He has had draw backs; he built bridges to link them all and then marched resolutely across. He has had defeats; he lives to fight again and again.

It is so easy to read an account of a man's life, seeing one victory after another, seeing the height he has attained from whence he started and think that he just breezed through life smelling like a rose and soldiering on like a saint, but the truth is that life is not that easy or that simple. One puts oneself out there, taking the battering from the storms of life, knowing that at the end of one storm, one will definitely be stronger and better prepared for the next storm already on the horizon. Then there are times when we don't swim against the current, but leave ourselves to float, allowing it to move us, as and when it will, but all the while surreptiously and silently paddling gently towards the shore and safety. Knowing the difference between when to stand up and fight or sound the call to fall back is a very fine line, because some of the greatest defeats or hugest victories were always against the largest odds and a split decision; on a wing and a prayer.

Who can say if a thing embarked on will end in success or failure? Sometimes hardwork and perseverance don't equate to success; sometimes one has to stand back, let go and let God, and yet there are times when one moves swiftly and confidently to the battle, aggressively ready for the ultimate sacrifice if that is what is required. Yes, time and chance do happen to all men.

Yet it takes faith and love to produce the pearl, as well as the motivation from the irritation that prompts one to take the decision to start making the pearl. We start our journey of life ignorant, crude, unread, uncivilized and untested, but above all, we start faithless and without confidence. It is the constant battering that life so cruelly and relentlessly brings against us that either destroys us or makes us stronger, better, learned, confident, civil, tried and tested. At every level of our growth and development, we face challenges that threaten to destroy, but it is in either the standing or the falling that we are able to move ever forward. It is expedient for us therefore to stand and fall as the situation demands; we must learn to toe the fine line, listen to the silent voice that tells us when to fight or refrain from fighting. It is, after all, this cruel and unrelenting life that ultimately is our best friend and teacher.

Akin's journey speaks of his desire and pursuit of constant growth and development; it is a story about career, giving, focus, courage, steadfastness, dignity, grace, hardwork, love, faith and the belief in his gifts. It shows that there will always be obstacles and we must prepare for and solve them. It shows that whoever we come across, we can touch, hopefully for the better. It shows that sometimes things can be so difficult to get and at other times, they just fall into one's lap. It is a story as compelling as any, yet it differs in many respects. The detail may vary but the general theme remains the same; life has to be lived authentically and faithfully, emotionally, passionately, fearlessly and to the full, selflessly giving oneself whenever called upon. Akin has found great joy in helping others, in his words,

> "...we must, wherever we find ourselves, create an atmosphere of selfless service..."

Yet, Akin, for all his growth and development, has remained ever constant, the same fun loving, excited with life, loyal, hardworking and hard playing man who has changed little from his Warri days. He is the friend best known to his inner circle of friends, as one who works hard and parties hard. He is known to his colleagues at work as the great motivator, initiator, mentor and philanthropist. Akin has taken his irritations and just like the oyster, he settled down and did what the oyster does best, better than any other creature. Akin turned them into pearls; beautiful and precious pearls, everyone of them.

"Success is to be measured not so much by the position that one has reached in life as by the obstacles which he has overcome while trying to succeed."

– Booker. T. Washington.

CHAPTER THIRTEEN

The Renaissance Man

"Hell begins on the day when God grants us a clear vision of all that we might have achieved, of all the gifts which we have wasted, of all that we might have done which we did not do…"

– *Gian-Carlo Menotti.*

After spending twenty seven purposeful and productive years in selfless service to Lagos State, Akin Ambode retired meritoriously, quietly and without fanfare, hoping to spend the rest of his productive years as a private citizen, living, growing and working in the private sector. A decision thought of as insane by some, and politically motivated by others, Akin refused to be swayed, second-guessed, frightened or intimidated at what the future would hold and what he should do. He bravely yet single mindedly set about in his trademark disciplined manner, the course that his retirement would take. His would not be the retirement of a tired and spent old man wishing to return to the village and play at farming; neither would it be one in which he would wake at noon, socialize idly with buddies at a club and babysit grandchildren. Akin, still in the full blush of his productive years, embarked on an action packed and fully charged 'second life'. This was going to be his chosen retirement plan, as 'taking things easy' or inactivity of any kind was just not going to be on the cards.

As anyone knows, spending such an uninterrupted length of time totally absorbed in one profession and in a particular sector would cause one to become slightly outdated with the current happenings in another sector. Lagos is such a dynamic, ever changing, constantly challenging organism that anyone living and working in her domain needs to always be on their toes and bring their best game forward to survive. Public service generally causes complacency and even though Akin always remained in touch with happenings outside the service, the sheer volume of work he put in while he was in service took its toll. He recognized at retirement that to take his next steps would require some measure of retraining and retooling and as a great believer in multi-tasking; he knew he would not have the luxury of taking several years off to go back to school and do things the traditional way.

The Renaissance man in him devised an exceptionally strategic plan, a retirement holiday package by which he would venture into the world of the modern scholar and he knew how best to accomplish this. He decided to earmark four different Ivy League business schools across the globe as a retirement gift to himself. This would bring him up to date with cutting edge finance and business processes and open him up to a whole new world of possibilities. It would also give him the opportunity to increase his human capital base by connecting with fellow scholars around the world with similar passions for business. Having spent so long in the world of finance, he knew he would always be in the business of numbers. Living requirements and family obligations, not to mention his passion for helping people and financing good causes, would require him to earn something substantial enough to cover all these competing interests. Starting out after so many years in Public service would also require substantial funds to set up an office and hire staff.

Having decided on the path his retirement would take, he packed his bags once again and headed for the 21st century lecture theatre and the business schools of the world to bring him up to date with the rest of the world. Some might have decided on a cruise, a spa holiday or some other luxury ending to a high octane Public service career, not so for Akin and this in a sense sums up the character of this man; always looking for the next challenge on the horizon and never backing down from something that requires great effort, it takes a special kind of person to go back to school mid-life, when they could be coasting at the top of their game.

It would be interesting to know what people facing this kind of transition should address their minds to, especially because retirement is always perceived as the end of productive life. What lessons can be learnt from Akin? His answers were most instructive:

> *"I think you need to know what the story of your life is all about; what roads you have walked down, what victories you have won, those you have lost and what lessons you have learnt from your victories and losses. You need to know what your strengths and weaknesses are and how they have shaped your life. You need to assess how many lives you have improved in whatever ways and how many you have empowered to be the best version of themselves, but above all, you need to know that your true value, your true wealth is measured not by the abundance of the material things you have gathered, but by the depth and quality of your humanity. It is so easy to focus solely on the self, its advancement and achievements and lose sight of everyone else, yes, even our most beloved ones. That makes us become so self centered that we turn into an idol that others worship and build their lives around. In the end we have no freedom but are bound by other peoples' expectations of us. One becomes enslaved by one's own egotistic appetite. The main task of life is to start early to find your concentric point of happiness and live your life around your happy settings, always having other peoples' wellbeing in mind and living with*

> *integrity; every other thing that is good will attract itself to you. It is not always about our capabilities and riches, but also about those things that bring joy and happiness to us every day; sometimes the little things we tend to undermine or overlook. Some of these things are right in front of us; the joy of our relationship with family, the beautiful friendships of our school days, the rich legacy of the various schools and institutions that prepared us for life's challenges, the business community that sharpens our talents and gifts, our native communities that have imbued us with a unique sense of culture and tradition, our nation that has given us an unshakable and indomitable identity. We find that these are the building materials from where we have come; we must understand our personal and collective callings and be true to same."*

So what next does this Renaissance man have up his sleeve? Akin looking confidently ahead laid down his mission as he sees it:

> *"...as I go into the future seeking to uncover what comes up next in my unfolding story, my mind is made up – to live from cradle to grave in happiness."*

What a fitting way to sum up the expectations for rest of one's life!

> *"The happiness which brings enduring worth to life is not the superficial happiness that is dependent on circumstances. It is the happiness and contentment that fills the soul even in the midst of the most distressing*

circumstances and the most bitter environment. It is the kind of happiness that grins when things go wrong and smiles through tears. The happiness for which our souls ache is one undisturbed by success or failure, one which will root deeply inside us and give inward relaxation, peace and contentment, no matter what the surface problems may be. That kind of happiness stands in need of no outward stimulus."

– Billy Graham.

CHAPTER FOURTEEN

Exceptional Extracurricular Expeditions

"Truly, I see hope…"

– Akin Ambode.

In addition to his stellar career in the Public service, Akin was constantly serving everywhere he could. His love for his alma mater, Federal Government College Warri is unparalleled. He served as Chairman of the Lagos Chapter of his Old Students Association (Fegocowosa) and did same in such a dedicated and committed way that he enkindled the interest of legions of members, inspiring them to also come on board and do something for the school. Under his administration, the Lagos Chapter became the most vibrant and financially solid of all the chapters. In his trademark way, he totally reorganized the workings of the Association by embarking on several team building and strengthening activities. He started 'Fegocowosa', the Lagos Chapter magazine in 2004, a high quality annual publication and in this maiden publication he exhorted former students with his own take on what old students should do. In his words, he stated that, *"True Fegocolians build bridges, not walls."*

The magazine highlighted the lives of former students, informed all members of the activities of the Association in the previous year and proposed activities of the current year, entertained with jokes, cartoons, recipes and anecdotes, handled pertinent and topical issues in the country and in education and provided a platform for integration and discourse. In his 2005 column titled, 'I See Hope', he passionately appealed to former students to do all they can to help. In his words,

> *"It is the task of Fegocowosa to set the tone for the restoration of our lost academic glory in Federal Government College Warri in particular and all Unity schools in general and by implication, in the entire country by involving all old students of other Unity Schools as we have already envisioned. We must see to it that the Fegocowosa journal is adequately supported as an effective communication link that will not only bond us together but will become a useful tool in communicating the need to revisit the ideals of Unity Schools by the relevant authorities as well as serve as an inspiration to members to address the compelling subject of leadership challenges in this country."*

Little did he know that this publication would find its way all over the world, everywhere there were former students and they in turn, would be inspired to set up foreign chapters of the Association in their countries of residence. The U.K. and U.S. Chapters of Fegocowosa were both born and nurtured by Akin's several visits and encouragement, along with several dedicated members resident in those countries.

He didn't stop at just monthly meetings, magazines, family day celebrations, Christmas parties, Founder's Day activities and encouraging support for a vibrant Cricket club for the Association; he became one of the voices crying out for a total rehabilitation of the school that after years of decay and neglect, had become a sad shadow of its former self. A school that had been a centre of excellence; that had produced an amazing number of highly qualified, well respected and truly exceptional leaders in all walks of life and in all professions, a school that had once had the honour of being the best in the West African sub-Region, but sadly had been so neglected that its condition shocked its alumni into action. Akin set out to bring together a team of former students that would explore the best way to put the school back to its former glory. In his 2006 column titled, 'The Future Is Ours', he philosophically examined why he was so passionate about his old school. In his words,

> *"Why am I passionate about our alma mater? The main objective of setting up Unity Schools is being*

realized through each and every one that passed through them. That objective is to raise young Nigerians who will uphold the unity of the country above all other considerations. Let us get it right, we are entirely a different breed from others, we are totally detribalized, tolerant in outlook, trained to accommodate others and their visions, irrespective of political, social, religious and ethnic dispositions. We are just what the future needs in Nigeria. There is no gainsaying that this is truly what Nigeria needs at the moment. Nigeria is in dire need of people who will appreciate its very abundant human and natural resources, people who will appreciate its strength in diversity, people to whom places of birth (a coincidence of which none of us actually had a choice) should be inconsequential in making national decisions, but at the time, people, who as brothers and sisters, would naturally elect to aid weaker siblings to greater heights without any feeling or cries of being drawn back. What society lacks and what we products of F. G. C. Warri and indeed all other Unity Schools have in abundance is love for one another. A brother will not be up there and be happy to see his siblings wallow in abject poverty. That is not true love. Nigeria at this moment more than any other time needs leaders who love the country and whose utmost desire is to share this love among the children of Nigeria. To many who never had the opportunity of sharing our experience, this vision is impossible, but for us products of F.G.C.Warri and products of Unity Schools, it is a very natural thing. It is for these reasons I strongly believe, that the future of this country, is indeed in our hands. The future is truly ours!"

In 2007, Akin had become the Chairman, Board of Patrons of the magazine. He was working tirelessly behind the scenes while several former students of F.G.C.Warri and former students of other Unity Schools, passionate titans of similar vision, worked in the fore front to come up with a National Ombudsman to champion the cause of qualitative education for all Nigerian children. He saw that his vision for his alma mater was one that had merit, but was myopic; he had to enlarge the vision to encompass the entire country so that no child would be left behind. First to be birthed was the Pro Unitate Forum; this took off informally in January 2006 with a series of meetings and a flurry of activity. It was formally registered as USOSA (Unity Schools Old Students Association) and duly incorporated as a Trustee comprising all alumni of 100 Unity Schools in Nigeria, with former students of FGC Sokoto, Enugu and Warri driving the process. The main thrust of the vision of USOSA is primarily dedicated to promoting the interest of Unity Schools. Specifically, USOSA provides a National platform through which alumni can focus on rekindling and sustaining the vision of the Founders of the Unity School concept as centres of academic excellence, integration, leadership and unity as well as influencing policy changes in the way and manner these schools are administered.

In his 2007 column titled, 'The Future Is Now!' Akin was unequivocal and as passionate as he had always been. Excited by the strides that USOSA was making, he postulated,

"That our school is a shadow of its former self is not news; this is a school that has produced men and women of incredible aptitude and abilities, who in their daily lives across the globe and here at home, are carrying the torch of excellence, hardwork, honesty, dignity of labour and unity. We have come to embody all that is worthy and good about Nigeria. However, our young brothers and sisters, who are presently students of FGCW and other Unity Schools, are bearing the brunt of the problems in the educational sector. They deserve better than what they are getting. The time has come when each of us must ask ourselves what we are doing to help. What are you contributing towards the rebuilding effort of FGCW and other Unity Schools? Time? Money? Effort? Moral support? What is your contribution? You cannot afford to fold your arms and watch as our schools crumble and decay. The young ones presently in Unity Schools are our future and the future of our country. If we want to see things change, improve and progress we must start sowing these seeds into their lives. We must fight for quality education for them, better standards, better opportunities, more books, dedicated teachers, excellent facilities and so on. We must aim to give them what we had and more to secure their future and the future of this country. They are the real heroes in this struggle because they find the courage to face the decay of our schools on a daily basis. Our founding fathers that set up the Unity School system fought for us to have excellent education knowing that the country would reap the benefits in years to come. It seems to me that we are on the threshold of another independence; this time not from a colonial master, but from a culture of

> *decadence, corruption, mediocrity, dishonesty and tribalism. We are the new 'founding fathers' of a nation of new hope; a Nigeria of honesty and unity, a Nigeria of brotherhood and progress. A Nigeria that is willing to make sacrifices to ensure that all those who previously bent their heads in shame can hold their heads up high, hand on heart and proclaim, 'Yes! I am Nigerian and proud to be!' I invite you to be part of the great and positive future, the time is now!"*

In 2010, Akin became the National President of the Old Students Association (Fegocowosa), in charge of all the Chapters both within and outside the country. He set about strengthening all the chapters by encouraging Chapter Chairmen to increase attendance at monthly meetings, by sourcing for funds to help rebuilding efforts at the school, by encouraging closer ties with USOSA, using his time, money and effort to help former students who were experiencing hard times by spearheading the launching of a Welfare Fund and so many other laudable efforts. In his 2008 column, he posed several questions,

> *"Why do we have such hopelessness on our streets? Why do we see such unpatriotic behaviour, such naked sabotage permeating every strata of our society? Why have we let go of optimism? Why have we traded faith for greed? Why have we dropped the ball? Why have we jettisoned service for self service?"*

Even in the face of overwhelming odds, Akin always looks on the bright side; he is a self confessed prisoner of hope. He does his best never to give in despair, because his training as both a Christian and a Humphrey Fellow are diametrically opposed to hopelessness. He prefers to see the silver lining around the dark cloud and focus on that till the darkness dissipates and light pours forth. He continued,

> *"In a country like Nigeria, we will find that things never go the way we want them to, we will find that something or someone will always throw a spanner in the works. That is just life, it is not meant to be perfect; there is no such thing and when we find ourselves in or with less than perfect circumstances, what we are meant to do is make the best of a bad job. Easier said than done, but thank God for the storms of life, thank God for the floods, for the traffic, for the lack, all these occurrences are designed for us to come into our own; to serve, to help our brothers and sisters get up, to rise, to step up to the plate and be counted. It is with this in mind that we are launching our Welfare Fund in Fegocowosa; how many will give of themselves and their resources to make this project a success? Will you be found wanting? Will you help to improve the lives of your fellow old students and by so doing, improve the lot of several dependants, family members, staff plus beneficiaries of their projects funded by your sacrifice and service? It is time for collective responsibility and service; let's make today and everyday a day in which we give thanks for what we have and are and a day to serve."*

Not content with all he has done and continues to do in Fegocowosa and on other platforms, Akin founded the La Roche Leadership Foundation in February 2013. Having always been concerned about the plight of education in Nigeria in general, he had spent several years in the past informally funding the development of qualitative education by supporting many educational establishments in cash and kind.

He also has a consuming passion for passing on leadership skills to younger people and spent several years unknowingly mentoring so many young people. The two passions; quality education and leadership training, he finally unified into one all-encompassing mission, the expression of which has culminated in the La Roche Leadership Foundation; a vehicle through which he hopes to touch the lives of as many children and young people as will avail themselves of the services of the Foundation.

Akin has been many things to many people and no doubt, he still has many caps that he will wear well in the rest of his life time. However, without a doubt, the one he has worn really well time and time again and continues to wear is his service cap; service, selfless service is an abiding part of his psyche and his conduct. He essentially is a man of selfless service.

> *"Let go of your ego today and join hands as we use our resources, our talents, our will and everything we have to move our less fortunate youth, old students, our fellow Lagosians and our fellow Nigerians out of hopelessness and despair and into optimism, faith and hope."*
>
> *– Akin Ambode.*

CHAPTER FIFTEEN

The Bare Essentials

"If all my pain and all my tears,
And all that I have learned throughout the years
Could make one perfect song
To lift some fallen head
To light some darkened mind,
I should feel that not in vain
I served mankind."

– Marguerite Few.

So what then is the art of selfless service? In the prologue, it was postulated that selfless service required seven essentials: Courage, Time, Effort,

Persistence, Patience and Focus, Love and Charity and lastly, Vision. To recap from the prologue:

> *'Selfless service takes courage; because most times the magnitude of what needs to be done can be daunting, time; because things once started must be seen through to a conclusive end no matter how long that takes. It takes effort; because the easy way out always leads to mediocrity and mediocrity never suffices, it takes persistence; because life has a way of throwing up road blocks in the most unexpected ways. It takes patience and focus; because things never go the way we plan them; life throws us curve balls and we need to roll with the punches. It takes love and charity; because no one can serve without loving the people that you serve even when they are unlovable and cruelly criticize everything, without looking at the merits of one's vision. Moreover it takes vision; because one must see the end from the beginning, so to speak.'*

Perhaps it is necessary to say a little more about each of these seven essentials and see from Akin's life how he fulfilled his art of selfless service.

Selfless service takes courage; in our reality, the courage to get the job done is in short supply. We tend to shrink away and remain with the crowd when tough jobs come up. Talk, which is said to be cheap, comes easy to us, so we talk and talk and talk when the job at hand needs swift and decisive action and most times to take that action requires strong courage. Akin always showed courage; when his father passed away so suddenly when he was young, when he could not get the job he thought he really wanted in the private sector, when he saw his dreams crumbling due to a fraud in the office where he first worked, but especially towards the end of his career as a Permanent Secretary and Accountant General heading the State Treasury Office. Imagine being in sole charge of the finances of the most populous state of the most populous African nation; being accountable to the present and past Governors of the State, who demanded excellence, being accountable to the thousands of public servants who rely on the STO for their financial direction and their budget, being accountable to the millions who call Lagos State their home; this is no small feat. Few people in this position can do this and meritoriously so.

Selfless service takes time; working with Akin was always a challenge going by all the interviewees testimonies; he was always acutely time conscious to the point where he used multi-tasking as his way to get around the constraints time forced on him. As succinctly put by Mrs. Yemisi Adams of the STO, *"Most days our colleagues in other ministries close by 4:00pm, while we are here till 8:00pm. Not because we get any over time, because we don't, but because of the work environment here and the way Mr. Akin is. He leads by example, he is a real leader...He likes things being done promptly; he doesn't like people waiting so long to be attended to."* And by Mr. Hakeem Alimi, also of the STO when he said, *"...he believes we must deliver, not waste time in treating an* issue. He has trained us not to waste time because as he says, you never know the urgency of something awaiting your attention."

Selfless service takes effort; Mr. Taiwo Wakeel found this out about Akin's philosophy on effort; he said, "*When I first came here, I was afraid of him and I would sometimes dodge him to avoid being near him. Then, he was always complaining about the state of cleanliness. But when I understood his style, that his standards are very high and once you can raise yours, you will have nothing to fear; then I stepped up the level of my work.*" As did Miss. Kemi Toso-Gbangba, "*… I feel he is a workaholic; he believes in getting the job done… He is prim, proper and believes in perfection…*" However, Akin is not just interested in expending effort; he wants results to be the end product of effort. This can be seen in his innovative spirit, where even in a place like the Public service, well known for strict protocol and unending bureaucracy, he was never afraid to convince his superiors of the need to improve on service delivery, targets, performance and the office environment so that all effort expended yields results. Again, Mr. Taiwo Wakeel; "*You can see that the State Treasury Office looks different from any other place in this facility, it looks just like a private sector office and we have everything we need here to be efficient and effective. This is how Mr. Ambode has made it so that we work here very well. Personally, I think he is guided by God to move the STO forward. Being in charge of the finance of the State Government is the most difficult job in the State* *service. We have to work with all other ministries and departments and our work is much more than others. If you work with Mr. Ambode you can be assured of two things: one, you will work very hard and two, you will close late. He makes us achieve set goals and targets and he has completely changed the way I used to work, because when you work with a hard worker, you will also have to work hard."*

Selfless service takes persistence; with the varied and many distractions that assault our senses daily, coupled with the barrage of negative news that occupies our conscious state, it is a wonder that anything can be successfully completed. We see our governments change policies and positions so frequently that implementation either lags far behind or drops off somewhere completely forgotten. On the other hand, we see innovations happening in more developed countries and have to wait agonizingly long periods before we get on the same page and enjoy the same great and new ways of getting things done efficiently and effectively. Akin always brought his A-game to the table with him; even when others thought it would be impossible to innovate, he always believed he could get the job done. That persistence was rewarded by moving up so rapidly through the public service ranks. Little wonder that before he was 50 years old, he had reached the peak of his career.

Selfless service takes patience and focus; we see this when he decided to take on his ICAN Certification, Master's degree and still work full time as well. We also see this when he was moving from one Local Government Office to the other; he saw each posting as an opportunity to learn and grow, not as a nuisance and a disruption. It is so easy to become impatient, resentful and feel unappreciated when serving especially in Local Government service, where being at the grassroots and on the frontline, one has to perform effectively and efficiently with little or no investment in human capital and infrastructure and with very meager resources. Akin's style was always to use what he had to get what he needed and leave behind a better way of doing things. He remained focused on the job and on achieving his goals and targets.

Selfless service takes Love and Charity; one of the hallmarks of Akin's service was his love for his work and charity to his colleagues' and staff. Akin's love for his work kept him in the office long after others had closed and gone home. His love for his work made him explore different ways he could improve himself so as to offer more. His love for his work kept him in the Public service instead of leaving for far more lucrative pastures in the private sector or even abroad in developed economies. The opportunities were there to later move, but he loved his work in the Public service more. His love for his work made him move to more challenging areas when he had mastered and conquered where he was at. His consuming passion was always to perform at the highest level of competence first. This is evident in the year he spent in Boston, working and studying as a Hubert Humphrey scholar. Only someone with a deep love for human beings and a passion to improve the human condition would subject themselves to a whole year of service in a foreign country. A big part of the Humphrey year involves working with the less privileged and in communities where there are great needs and deprivation, doing whatever is required to improve things and solve problems. Humphrey scholars stand out because the programme makes them sensitive to the needs of others. It is not a comfortable or glamorous programme, but one that deeply satisfies the need to be a helper.

His charity to others was and still is an integral part of him; everywhere he has worked, he was and is known to have a large heart. He demonstrated this with his love and passion for his alma mater, Federal Government College Warri and in the many offices he has held in the Old Students Association, in which he dedicated himself wholeheartedly to several causes to bring progress to the school and members of the Association on state, national and international level. He continues today to be continually concerned about this progress. His founding of the *La Roche Leadership Foundation* also shows his huge heart of charity and his dedication to uplifting the most vulnerable members of the society.

Mr. Hakeem Alimi referred to his charity as his secret when he said, *"It is my opinion that one of the secrets to his success is his charity; his compassion and love for people. God has given him a huge capacity for empathy, to put himself in other peoples' shoes; he is a great helper and forgives wrongs so easily. Not many people have the heart to be charitable; it is a gift from God.*" and Mrs. Yemisi Adams said, "*...Personally, it is because I came here that I got my professional degree; the first time I got here, we had a meeting with Mr. Akin and he challenged us all to be more professional, to grow and be better Accountants. That was when I made up my mind to go ahead and do my ICAN. He also supported me when I wanted to travel and encouraged me to think bigger. He doesn't like bragging about what he does, he does things very quietly. He helps whoever comes across him, not minding tribe, sex or religion.*" Perhaps Mr. Taiwo Wakeel put it best when he said, "*...Around the STO, we call him 'Baba Laanu'; he has great goodwill with all staff...*" Roughly translated it means 'Father of Mercy'. What a moving description of charity one could learn something from.

Lastly, selfless service takes vision; being able to see what is not yet manifest, seeing how a thing will turn out when one has not yet started, having faith in one's imagination and the ability to bring into being the thing imagined; an abstract concept, but one that every visionary must have. Akin's visions of the what, where, how and why's of his life's work took great vision, one has to not mind the everyday irritations and problems. Looking back at his twenty seven year career, one might be tempted to think that the doors that were open to him were all in place, but as we know, hindsight has 20/20 vision; the truth is that no one can definitely say how a thing will turn out, one just does one's selfless best, believing in one's gifts and hoping for the best. Akin walked in his visions, remaining true to them even when others could not see the merit in or reward for them; as a visionary, he didn't let the reality of what was before him make him let go of his visions, rather he clung to them and brought them into reality.

Vision in selfless service therefore requires all the other essentials to be holistically in operation; Courage, Time, Effort, Persistence, Patience and Focus, Love and Charity and lastly, Vision. These are therefore, the bare essentials of the art of selfless service.

> *"I long to accomplish a great and noble task, but it is my chief duty to accomplish humble tasks as though they were great and noble. The world is moved along, not only by the mighty shoves of its heroes, but also by the aggregate of the tiny pushes of each honest worker."*
>
> *– Helen Keller.*

Epilogue

"Let us then think only of the present, and not even permit our minds to wander with curiosity into the future. This future is not yet ours; perhaps it never will be. It is exposing ourselves to temptation, to wish, to anticipate God, and to prepare ourselves for things which he may not destine for us. If such things should come to pass, he will give us light and strength according to need. Why should we desire to meet difficulties prematurely, when we have neither strength nor light as yet provided for them? Let us give heed to the present whose duties are pressing; it is fidelity to the present which prepares us for fidelity in the future."

– Francois Fenelon.

Sometimes one must allow the indulgence of one's mind to wander into the unknown future, for the past, once past cannot be corrected, the present, which we live in now, can become crowded with wants, needs, whys and why not's, but the future provides us with the means to fantasize about the direction in which we wish to go and grow, even if we are unable in reality to dictate the pace or direction of even one second of our future. It is said that a man who dreams can create, a man who dreams big can create big and a man who does not dream is dead.

Akin has always dreamt big; from his innocent and childlike beginnings at St. Jude's Primary School, when the little boy Akin first started his educational journey, to the vastly well read, supremely confident and mature man completing his final assignment in public service at the STO, he has always had high hopes and big dreams. All along his journey, the constant themes that have marked his life and times are his penchant for not settling for the comfortable, his determination to see things through to their successful end, his inability to accept the mediocre, his refusal to back down from challenges, his dissatisfaction with excuses, his unwillingness to conform to low standards or the unsatisfactory norm, his unhappiness with selfishness and waste, his strict attitudes to integrity and honesty, his deep commitment to keeping his word and his profound humility. Throughout his journey, he has built layer upon layer of the principles that have served him well and has proved time and time again that he can perform when called upon at the highest level of competence.

Akin still dreams big dreams; he dreams of a time when excellence will be commonplace, when people will naturally do the right things at the right time. He dreams of a time when everyone will have and keep the right perspective, when those in public office will serve as they are meant to serve, selflessly for the benefit of all. He dreams of a time when those in private office will willingly seek out ways to partner with governments on projects that will help the most vulnerable in society and do so sacrificially, not consumed with what they can gain in return. He hopes for a time when the grassroots of society will be judged as important as every other strata of society in terms of opportunities, infrastructure and in deliverables. He dreams of an orderly, disciplined and integrity driven society that realizes its place in history and remains true to its calling. He dreams that the mistakes of the past will serve as a wakeup call for those in the present and a blue print for the youth in the future. He dreams of a better tomorrow, a tomorrow where everyone did their best today to make a difference; for he is the quintessential Humphrey man, for him, everyone can and must make a difference.

Akin still dreams big and he will likewise continue to create big, because dreamers never really die. The present Dalai Lama, on visiting the site where Rev. Martin Luther King was shot, commented that even if a dreamer is killed, his dreams can still live on, but if we say a dream lives on and becomes reality, then the dreamer cannot be said to be dead. Akin has, in his time so far, dreamt dreams and created several realities. Having reached the beginning of a new chapter in his life, he remains resolutely fixed on courageously stepping out into the unknown future; the past, with all its challenges, hardships and victories behind him and the future stretched ahead, hidden and unknown. For now, the present, one can only wish that those big dreams of his all come to pass the way he has dreamt them.

> *"I have no yesterdays,*
> *Time took them away;*
> *Tomorrow may not be –*
> *But I have today."*
>
> *– Pearl Yeadon Mc Ginnis.*

Index of Quotations

Benjamin Franklin…pg xi

Henry Drummond…pg xiv

Alan Beck…pg 1

Angelo Patri…pg 4

John Ruskin…pgs 5, 27, 79

Frank Dempster Sherman…pg 14

James Freeman Clarke…pg 15

Burnett H Streeter…pg 19

Washington Gladden…pg 21

Phillip Brooks…pg 29

George Hodges…pg 33

Pamela Vaull Starr…pg 35

Akin Ambode…pgs 49, 62, 73, 90, 91, 93, 94, 95, 101

The Living Age…pg 41

Hubert Horatio Humphrey…pg 47

Geraldine Chin…pg 52

James Russell Lowell…pg 53

Eleanor Roosevelt…pg 59

Johann Wolfgang Von Goethe…pg 61

Lucy Larcom … pg 75

Harry Emerson Fosdick…pg 81

Booker T Washington…pg 85

Gian-Carlo Menotti…pg 87

Billy Graham…pg 91

Marguerite Few…pg 103

Helen Keller…pg 111

Francois Fenelon…pg 113

Pearl Yeadon McGinnis…pg 116

Acknowledgements

The Treasure Chest by Charles L Wallis, Harper & Row, Publishers.

The Concise Oxford Dictionary 5th Edition by Oxford At The Clarendon Press.

Fegocowosa Magazine issues: 2004, 2005, 2006, 2007, 2008.

Developing The Total Nigerian Child; Quality And Unity Driven by Federal Government College Warri, Old Students Association.

Federal Government College Warri – The Rise And Fall Of An Institution Of Excellence by Federal Government College Warri, Old Students Association.

Family Values: What Part Do They Play In Our Society? By Marina Osoba.

The Hubert Horatio Humphrey Fellowship Program.

The American Fulbright Scholarship Program at Boston University, Massachusetts, U.S.A.

The State Treasury Office; Ministry Of Finance, Lagos State Secretariat, Alausa, Ikeja.

The Institute of Chartered Accountants of Nigeria, Lagos State Public Service Chapter and Mr. Sakirudeen Odusanya.

Business Day Media Ltd.

Mrs. Yemisi Adams, Mr. Taiwo Wakeel, Mr. Hakeem Alimi, Miss Oluwakemi Toso-Gbangba, Mrs. Olumuyiwa Ojelabi, Mr. Osinubi Olalekan and Mr. Bunmi Ariyo.

About the Author

Marina Sukuta Osoba attended Federal Government College, Warri for both O and A Levels and studied Law at the University of Lagos. A Solicitor and Advocate of the Supreme Court of Nigeria since 1989, she writes mainly poetry. She is presently the Administrator of the La Roche Leadership Foundation, a non-profit organisation concerned with education and leadership training for children and young people.

She is also a columnist for Takaii, a legal magazine; Joy, a women's lifestyle interest magazine; Fegocowosa, a magazine for and about alumni of her old school, Federal Government College, Warri, and is a volunteer teacher of an adult creative writing class for Poise Nigeria Limited.

She is married to Mr. Mike Ade Osoba and has four children. Her hobbies include writing, cookery, photography, reading and she is proficient in various crafts like crochet, knitting and macrame.

www.ingramcontent.com/pod-product-compliance
Lightning Source LLC
Chambersburg PA
CBHW071412300426
44114CB00016B/2278